Marian Cox

# Cambridge IGCSE®

# First Language English

## Workbook

### Fourth edition

CAMBRIDGE
UNIVERSITY PRESS

# CAMBRIDGE
## UNIVERSITY PRESS

University Printing House, Cambridge CB2 8BS, United Kingdom

Cambridge University Press is part of the University of Cambridge.

It furthers the University's mission by disseminating knowledge in the pursuit of education, learning and research at the highest international levels of excellence.

Information on this title: education.cambridge.org

First published 2003
Third edition 2010
Fourth edition 2014
6th printing 2016

Printed in Dubai by Oriental Press

ISBN 978-1-107-69577-1 Paperback

Additional resources for this publication at education.cambridge.org

Cambridge University Press has no responsibility for the persistence or accuracy of URLs for external or third-party internet websites referred to in this publication, and does not guarantee that any content on such websites is, or will remain, accurate or appropriate. Information regarding process, travel timetables and other factual information given in this work is correct at the time of first printing but Cambridge University Press does not guarantee the accuracy of such information thereafter.

® IGCSE is the registered trademark of Cambridge International Examinations.

The publisher is grateful to the following expert reviewers: Mair Lewis, Tony Parkinson.

.............................................................................................................................

# Contents

iv

# Introduction

This supplementary workbook is designed to support the coursebook Cambridge IGCSE First Language English by Marian Cox, fourth edition published by Cambridge University Press in 2014. The skills offered for practice are those examined in Cambridge IGCSE First Language English 0500/0522/0524, which are comprehension, writer's effects analysis, summary, directed writing, and composition. The texts in each unit are suitable for both core- and extended-tier candidates.

This workbook, which has been revised as part of the fourth edition IGCSE suite, contains 12 independent units, each based on a different topic, divided into the sections Language and Style, Comprehension and Summary, Directed Writing, and Composition or Coursework. (In some cases the titles could be used for either.) Each unit gives practice in the generic examination response techniques of skimming, scanning, selecting, collating and structuring. The topics have been selected to cater for a variety of interests and to have international appeal to the relevant age group. The passages cover the range of genres for reading and writing exam tasks. The tasks are intended as follow-up work to the coursebook (ISBN 9781107657823). They give further opportunities to practise the reading and writing skills and language points that are introduced or revisited in the matching coursebook unit.

The units are roughly equal in level of difficulty and can be studied in any order. Each unit contains a mixture of exam-type tasks for skills practice as well as specific language tasks on spelling, punctuation, vocabulary extension or grammar points. Teachers can select tasks according to which skills and language areas need practising at a particular time by a particular student or class. The contents page indicates which language-revision and exam-type practice tasks are contained in each unit.

Speaking and Listening skills are not directly addressed in this supplementary workbook, but many of the reading and directed writing tasks could be extended or adapted to become Speaking and Listening tasks for examination practice or internal assessment.

By using this workbook, students will become familiar with a range of exam-style passages and tasks and gain practice in writing in different voices and registers for different audiences. The tasks can be done in class, as homework, or by the student working independently. An Answers appendix gives suggested answers for tasks where appropriate, though these are not necessarily definitive. (The appendix can be removed from student copies of the workbook.) Answer space for all questions is given in the workbook, the size of the space indicating the expected length of the response.

# Unit 1: Rocket science

## A Reading

1    Read the letter below.

### Passage A: New Year's Eve fireworks

Dear Mum and Dad

Happy New Year! Hope you had a good New Year's Eve. I had the most amazing time here in Dubai, watching the biggest firework display ever – an **extravaganza** lasting six minutes, which set a new world record for a single **coordinated** display. The 500,000 fireworks were set off from 400 firing locations, **synchronised** by 100 computers. It took the **technicians** ten months to plan!

There was a countdown to midnight in fireworks in both roman and arabic numerals. Organisers said they wanted to create a burst of light to imitate a sunrise and dazzle spectators with a United Arab Emirates flag that could also break records for being the largest ever made of fireworks. They certainly did that!

I was down with thousands of watchers standing by the fountains at Burj Khalifa, the world's tallest tower, which was used as a backdrop for the display. Everyone got there early and the anticipation beforehand was **electric**; it wasn't only the children who were excited! The Burj is shaped like a rocket itself, and was the launch pad for thousands of smaller rockets. It was turned into a whole series of famous monuments, like the Eiffel Tower, by patterns of light flashing on it. And that was just a small part of it …

It was a helter-skelter, with showers of sparks sliding down it. It was an **incandescent** pine tree with thousands of starry branches. It was a castle unleashing arrows of fire. Down below there was an orchard of trees bursting into blossom; there were pulsing globes like dandelion heads sending out seeds; there were tiered birthday cakes with exploding candles. **Iridescent** rings climbed the tower. **Scintillating** fountains leapt up to meet the cascades of light. Bouquets of bright flowers of every hue filled the sky.

Everyone was holding up their phone to capture the images, holding their breath, mesmerised. It was too much to take in; there were too many places to look simultaneously. The soundtrack of sci-fi film-type music matched the display of dancing light and water, and made it a space-age experience. There was huge applause at the end, cheering and whistling that went on for ages. It was unforgettable, and I really wish you could have seen it too.

Maybe next year! I'm really enjoying the job and the lifestyle, so I'll still be here then!

Love
Lee

1

## B  Language and style

2   Give meanings for the following words, as they are used in Passage A. Look up any words you do not know, but first try to guess from the prefix or stem of the word.

a   extravaganza _____

b   coordinated _____

c   synchronised _____

d   technicians _____

e   electric _____

f   incandescent _____

g   iridescent _____

h   scintillating _____

i   mesmerised _____

j   simultaneously _____

3   a   Next to each of the above words, write which part of speech it is, as used in the passage.

    b   Study the words and then write out without looking (in a notebook) those you did not know how to spell.

## C  Comprehension and summary

4   Re-read the fourth paragraph of Passage A and comment on:

a   the sentence structure and its effect

_____

_____

_____

_____

b   the vocabulary and its effect

_____

_____

_____

_____

5   Select relevant material from the passage and write a news report, with a suitable headline,
    for the next day's local newspaper.

_____

_____

_____

_____

_____

_____

_____

_____

_____

_____

_____

_____

_____

_____

_____

_____

_____

_____

_____

_____

_____

_____

_____

# D Reading

**6** Read the following encyclopedia article.

## Passage B: Facts about fireworks

**F**ireworks are believed to have been invented more than 2000 years ago in China, where they were used in the form of firecrackers to accompany many festivities, in order to ward off evil and invoke prosperity. It is believed that the first firecrackers were actually accidental: chunks of bamboo thrown onto a fire. (Bamboo traps air inside the segments so that when heated it expands and bursts through the sides, and this could have started the idea.) China is the largest manufacturer and exporter of fireworks in the world; 90% of all fireworks originate from there. Firecrackers are still made by hand, and it is a hazardous job.

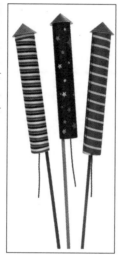

In 1240, the Arabs acquired knowledge of gunpowder, and in the same century firecrackers arrived in Europe, with the crusaders or Marco Polo. The key ingredient in making fireworks is gunpowder, which consists of saltpetre (potassium nitrate), charcoal and sulphur. Early fireworks were enjoyed less for the show than for the sound; simple gunpowder explodes quickly with a terrific bang but with <u>little</u> colour. Over time, people discovered that using chemical compounds with greater amounts of oxygen made the explosives burn brighter and longer. At first fireworks were only orange and white. In the Middle Ages, new colours were achieved by adding different minerals. They had <u>least</u> success with blue. This became available with the discovery of copper compounds, but this is an unstable metal and so is <u>less</u> frequently used.

It wasn't until the 1800s that fireworks developed into what we know today. Italy was the first country in Europe to truly master and experiment with pyrotechnics, by loading firecrackers into cannons and shooting them into the air. Multi-hued displays were an innovation of the 1830s, when metals that burn at high temperatures and create colours, sparks and noises were added to gunpowder. The Italians are still at the forefront of pyrotechnic development, and the phenomenal New Year display in Dubai in 2014 was masterminded by the Italian-American Phil Grucci.

Every year, people in China celebrate the invention of the firecracker on 18th April. Fireworks are also an integral part of the Chinese New Year celebrations. The big occasion for fireworks in the UK is Guy Fawkes Night (5th November) to celebrate the failure of the Gunpowder Plot to blow up parliament. France uses fireworks to celebrate Bastille Day, commemorating the storming of the prison during the French Revolution. Firework displays are also a major part of Independence Day celebrations in the United States.

The world record for the largest firework display before January 2014 in Dubai consisted of 77,282 fireworks set off in Kuwait in November 2011 as part of the country's 50th anniversary celebrations. The largest firework rocket –13 kg – was produced and launched in Portugal in 2010. The biggest annual firework display event in Europe is the International Festival concert held in Edinburgh, Scotland, in which no <u>fewer</u> than a million fireworks are set off in <u>less</u> than an hour. A string of firecrackers lasting 22 hours marked the New Year's Day celebrations in Hong Kong in 1996. The world's largest single firework was seen at a festival in Japan in 1988; the burst was over a kilometre across and the shell weighed over half a tonne. A rocket can reach speeds of 240 kph, and the shell can reach as high as 200 metres. People will always see the explosion of a firework before hearing it. This is because although they both travel in waves, light travels at 1080 million kph whereas sound travels only at 1225 kph.

In public shows today, specialists use computers to control the electronic ignition of fireworks, as well as to synchronise the aerial bursts with music. Firework displays are becoming ever more spectacular and are an established way of celebrating any global, national or local event or anniversary.

4

# E  Language and style

**7  a**  Underline the passive verb forms in Passage **B**.

**b**  Explain why passive rather than active verb forms are used in certain types of text.

_____

_____

_____

**8**  Look at the underlined words in Passage **B** and consider how they are used. Fill the blanks in the paragraph below with one of these words. (You may want to use some words more than once, and come not at all.)

| few | fewer | fewest | a few | little | less | least | a little |

There are _____ signs of fireworks losing popularity as a form of entertainment. Gradually,

private firework shows are becoming _____ common and are being replaced by public

events. This means that the injuries caused by fireworks are _____, but they are still

a cause of damage to property, unintended fires, maiming of children and traumatising of animals.

_____ people argue that fireworks are destructive in many senses, and that the expense and

waste of natural resources cannot be justified in return for _____ moments of pleasure,

but there is _____ public debate on the subject, and unlikely to be, given that they have

been around for so long.

**9**  Use *given that* (used in the last line of the paragraph above) correctly in a sentence of your own.

_____

_____

# F  Comprehension and summary

**10  a**  In which century did fireworks become known in Europe?

_____

**b**  Express in your own words what happened to fireworks in the 1830s.

_____

_____

_____

**c** Which country held the world record for a coordinated firework display before New Year's Eve 2014?

_____

**d** Explain in your own words why we see fireworks before we hear them.

_____

**e** Express the following phrases in your own words.

   **i**  invoke prosperity

_____

   **ii**  multi-hued displays were an innovation

_____

   **iii**  still at the forefront

_____

**11** **In one sentence each, summarise what Passage B says about:**

  **a**  the Chinese and fireworks

_____

_____

_____

  **b**  the Italians and fireworks

_____

_____

_____

  **c**  how fireworks are made

_____

_____

_____

**12** **Write a one-paragraph summary of the history of fireworks.**

_____

_____

_____

_____

_____

_____

## G  Directed writing

13  Write an article for a school magazine called 'Who needs fireworks?' Engage with some of the ideas and use some of the facts contained in Passages A and B in order to construct the argument that: 'too much money is wasted on this form of brief, childish and destructive entertainment'.

_____

_____

_____

_____

_____

_____

_____

_____

_____

_____

_____

_____

_____

_____

_____

_____

_____

_____

_____

_____

## H Composition

### Descriptive writing

**a** Describe the environment and atmosphere of a venue waiting for an exciting event to start.

**b** Give an account of a real or imaginary experience of witnessing a sensational show.

### Narrative writing

**c** Write a story which involves an explosion.

**d** Continue this story opening: 'I was really looking forward to the coming year ...'

**1** Discuss the competitiveness between countries to beat records and outdo each other, and say whether you think this is good for the world.

**2** 'New Year's Eve'. Write a short story with this title.

*Coursework topics*

# Unit 2: Bears and apes

## A Reading

1 Read the article below.

### Passage A: How the teddy got its name

A few people, perhaps of the kind who like to **amass** curious snippets of information, could probably tell you that the children's cuddly toy known as a 'teddy bear' is so called after Theodore ('Teddy') Roosevelt, who was President of the United States from 1901 to 1909. Far fewer could tell you just why a US President should have given his name to an object which by 1907 was selling almost a million a year.

All accounts are agreed upon the fact that early in life Roosevelt suffered from asthma and that his father believed that fresh air and exercise would improve his health. As a result, the future President became keen on outdoor pursuits and even studied to be a naturalist before taking up politics. However, he still continued to hunt, a very fashionable sport at the time.

And so it was that in 1902, while the President was taking time off from solving a border **dispute** in Mississippi, that the incident took place which linked his name for ever with the little furry creature. Roosevelt had had a bad day and shot nothing at all, so the guides, not wishing the **expedition** to be a failure, sent out dogs to track down a bear for the President to shoot. Here, however, accounts differ: some say that the black bear which they cornered was old and exhausted; others that it was a lost bear cub which was tracked down. Whichever was the case, Roosevelt refused to shoot it, saying that he considered this would be unsporting.

A political cartoonist called Clifford K. Berryman heard the story and made a drawing of the incident for the *Washington Post* (and in a second version of the cartoon he reduced the size of the bear, which may have given rise to the idea that it was a cub). The cartoon was so popular that Berryman depicted the young bear in other drawings of Roosevelt. The President's name was now firmly linked with bears, but how did his nickname of 'Teddy' come to be given to the toy bear? The owner of a New York toy shop, Morris Mitchom, asked the President if he could call the bears in his shop, which his wife made, 'Teddy's Bears', to which Roosevelt agreed. Mitchom then founded the Ideal Toy and Novelty Company, which was to become one of the biggest toy companies in the United States.

However, the Mitchoms were not the first to make toy bears. Richard Steiff, a member of a German family firm, invented a bear with jointed limbs in 1902. This he exhibited at the 1903 Leipzig Spring Fair. The creature was a metre high, fierce-looking and heavy, and had the effect of scaring off potential customers rather than attracting them – with the exception of an American importer, Borgfeldt, who thought he recognised a way of cashing in on the popularity of the bear in the Roosevelt story. He ordered 3000 of them: the teddy bear boom had begun.

Early examples of the teddy bear are now worth a fortune: a 1904 Steiff bear was sold for £110,000 in 1994.

Since then, generations of children – and adults – have been **entranced** by this domesticated version of one of nature's fiercest predators, now made of every possible material from wool and wood to modern **synthetics** such as nylon. The teddy has featured as the hero of immensely popular books such as *Winnie-the-Pooh*, *Rupert Bear*, *The Jungle Book* and the Paddington Bear series, and its image appears on keyrings, greetings cards, mugs, posters and charity logos. It is also used to draw attention to the problems of bears that today live in threatened habitats, perhaps the most fitting way of commemorating President Roosevelt's refusal – 100 years ago – to shoot a defenceless bear for 'sport'.

9

## B Language and style

2 Make sentences of your own which show the meaning of the words in bold in Passage **A**. Use a dictionary if you are not sure, but first try to work out their meaning from their context and their similarity to other words you already know.

**a** amass _____

_____

**b** dispute _____

_____

**c** expedition _____

_____

**d** entranced _____

_____

**e** synthetics _____

_____

3 Circle all the pairs of dashes, brackets and commas in Passage **A**. As you can see, they form a parenthesis (i.e. a word or phrase of comment or explanation inserted into a sentence which is grammatically complete without it). Commas are the most subtle, and brackets the least because of their visual impact.

Put a variety of parenthetical punctuation into the following sentences, considering how close you think the extra information is to the content of the main sentence. Some sentences may need more than one parenthesis.

**a** Wild apes have no need of language and have not developed it but tame ones can use it as a tool for communicating with each other.

**b** Each slaughtered ape is a loss to the local community a loss to humanity as a whole and is a hole torn in the ecology of our planet.

**c** The skills of language and counting essential for negotiating trade can be taught to orang-utans who are less social primates than chimpanzees in a matter of weeks.

**d** Fifteen million years a small gap in the broad scale of evolution is an immense period in terms of everyday life.

**e** Gorilla mothers prefer to cradle their babies on their left sides a feature shared with humans and there have been cases of them showing maternal behaviour to human children.

## C Comprehension and summary

**4** Say whether the following statements are true (T), false (F) or 'don't know' (D), and give reasons.

**a** More people know whom the bear is named after than know why.

_____

**b** Roosevelt was more of a hunter than a wildlife supporter.

_____

**c** The bear Roosevelt refused to shoot was a cub.

_____

**d** The Ideal Toy and Novelty Company was the first to manufacture teddy bears in the USA.

_____

**e** The customers at the Leipzig Spring Fair in 1903 found the bears very attractive.

_____

**5** **a** Highlight the material in Passage **A** that you would use to explain how the teddy got its name. Write each point separately below, in your own words as far as possible, ordering them logically.

_____

_____

_____

_____

_____

_____

_____

**b** Link the points to create no more than two sentences.

_____

_____

_____

_____

_____

_____

_____

## D Reading

**6** Read the story below.

## Passage B: A tale of a bear

There was once a lady who lived in an old manor house on the border of a big forest, high up in the North. This lady had a pet bear she was very fond of. It had been found in the forest half-dead of hunger, so small and helpless that it had to be brought up on the bottle by the lady and her old cook. This was several years ago and now it had grown up to be a big bear so strong that he could have slain a cow and carried it away if he had wanted to.

But he did not want to; he was a most amiable bear who did not dream of harming anybody, man or beast. He used to sit outside his kennel and look with his small, intelligent eyes most amicably at the cattle grazing in the field nearby. The children used to ride on his back and had more than once been found asleep in his kennel between his two paws. The three Lapland dogs loved to play all sorts of games with him, pull his ears and his stump of a tail and tease him in every way, but he did not mind in the least.

He had a fine appetite, but his friend the cook saw to it that he got his fill. Bears are vegetarians if they have a chance; fruit is what they like best. Bears look clumsy and slow in their movements, but try a bear with an apple tree and you will soon find out that he can easily beat any schoolchild at that game.

There had also been some difficulties about the bee-hives; he had been punished for this by being put on the chain for two days with a bleeding nose and he had never done it again. Otherwise he was only put on the chain at night (for a bear is apt to get somewhat ill-tempered if kept on a chain) or on Sundays when his mistress went to spend the afternoon with her married sister, who lived in a solitary house on the other side of the mountain lake, a good hour's walk through the dense forest. It was not considered good for him to wander about in the forest with all its temptations. Now he knew quite well what it meant when his mistress put him on the chain on Sundays, with a friendly tap on his head and the promise of an apple on her return if he had been good during her absence. He was sorry but resigned.

One Sunday when the lady had chained him up as usual and was about half-way through the forest, she suddenly thought she heard the cracking of a tree branch on the winding footpath behind her. She looked back and was horrified to see the bear coming along full-speed. In a minute he had joined her, panting and sniffing, to take up his usual place, dog-fashion, at her heels. The lady was very angry: she was already late for lunch, there was no time to take him back home, she did not want him to come with her, and besides, it was very naughty of him to have disobeyed her and broken away from his chain. She ordered him in her severest voice to go back at once, menacing him with her umbrella. He stopped a moment and looked at her with his cunning eyes, but then kept on sniffing at her. When the lady saw that he had even lost his new collar, she got still more angry and hit him on the nose with her umbrella so hard that it broke in two. He stopped again, shook his head, and opened his big mouth several times as if he wanted to say something. Then he turned round and began to shuffle back the way he had come, stopping now and then to look at the lady till at last she lost sight of him.

When the lady came home in the evening, he was sitting in his usual place outside his kennel looking very sorry for himself. The lady was still very angry with him and she told him that he would have no apple and no supper, and that he would be chained for two days as an extra punishment.

The old cook, who loved the bear as if he had been her son, rushed out from the kitchen. 'What are you scolding him for, missus?' she asked. 'He has been as good as gold the whole day, bless him! He has been sitting here looking the whole time towards the gate for you to come back.'

It had been a different bear!

## E Language and style

7   Write sentences about the bear in Passage **B** using ideas expressed in the following grammatical structures.

**a**   Not only … but also

_____

_____

**b**   Never before …

_____

_____

**c**   Neither … nor

_____

_____

**d**   No longer …

_____

_____

**e**   Not so much as a …

_____

_____

8   **a**   Explain how the writer achieves the effect of surprise in Passage **B**.

_____

_____

_____

_____

**b**   Explain how the writer evokes sympathy for the bear in Passage **B**.

_____

_____

_____

_____

_____

_____

**F** **Comprehension and summary**

9  a  Summarise the story of Passage **B** in one paragraph.

_____

_____

_____

_____

_____

_____

_____

_____

_____

_____

_____

_____

b  Give the reasons , in sentences, why humans find bears attractive, using ideas from Passages **A** and **B**.

_____

_____

_____

_____

_____

_____

_____

_____

_____

_____

_____

_____

_____

## G Directed writing

**10**   Read the information in the fact box below.

> **Great apes survival project**                                            **FACT**
>
> **Population:** over past 20 years, surveys indicate substantial and continual decline from 100,000 individuals reported in 1980
> **Habitat:** Cameroon and Congo basin and other central African equatorial regions; once virgin rainforest
> **Characteristics:** share 99% of human DNA; live for 60 years; capable of intelligent communication with the comprehension level of a six-year-old child; can learn sign language; have IQ of 80, similar to many humans
> **Threats:** hunters earn $35 for a dead male silverback gorilla; orphaned babies cannot survive; could be extinct in 5–10 years because of destruction of habitat and slaughter for cheap bush meat with snares and guns; commercial mining for coltan, used in mobile phones, games consoles and military aircraft, has already made some gorilla populations extinct
> **Aims:** appoint rangers ('ecoguards') and provide vehicles and communication equipment to monitor and protect animals; construct wildlife corridors to link fragmented habitats; educate locals on value of apes for eco-tourism; gain legal rights to protect apes and chimpanzees and their right to life and liberty, and to freedom from torture and medical experimentation, because of their similarity to humans

**11**   Write an informative article for your school magazine to explain the project.

_____

_____

_____

_____

_____

_____

_____

_____

_____

_____

_____

_____

_____

_____

_____

_____

_____

_____

_____

_____

_____

_____

_____

_____

_____

_____

_____

_____

_____

_____

_____

_____

**12**  **Read the following fact box about spectacled bears.**

## The spectacled bear campaign

FACT

**Population:** approx. 3000 left; population has collapsed because of destruction of rainforest during last 30 years

**Habitat:** around the Andes in South America, in cloud forests and Andean moorland; found in countries such as Venezuela, Argentina and Peru

**Characteristics:** only bear in this continent; also known as the Andean bear; has bands of colour around the eyes; shaggy fur; very shy; smaller than other bears; nocturnal; solitary; excellent climber; eats mainly fruit and nuts; sometimes carnivore; cubs born November–February in rainy season

**Threats:** bears frequently killed for sport or by farmers protecting crops; cubs sometimes captured and kept in appalling conditions for the amusement of their captors; discovered only in second half of 20th century; may disappear before end of the 21st century

**Aims:** to rescue bears from captivity in small cages and remove them to specially created sanctuaries

**Other information:** one of the causes adopted by the Rainforest Alliance

**13** Write a speech persuading students at your school to help raise funds for the spectacled bears.

_____

_____

_____

_____

_____

_____

_____

_____

_____

_____

_____

_____

_____

_____

_____

_____

_____

_____

_____

_____

_____

_____

# H Composition

## Descriptive writing

**a** 'The Circus'. Write a descriptive composition with this title.

**b** Describe an incident that occurred during a real or fictitious hunting or fishing expedition, and give your thoughts and feelings at the time.

## Narrative writing

**c** Write a story set in a place where there are wild animals.

**d** 'But it wasn't the same animal!' Write a story that ends with this sentence.

1 Write the words of a talk in which you argue that animals do or do not have rights.

2 Write a story in which a key role is played by an animal.

Coursework topics

# Unit 3: Simply flying

## A Reading

**1** Read the article below.

### Passage A: My life at TopFlights

It's 8.00 a.m. Monday morning, and Manchester Airport is closed due to fog. As a result three TopFlights flights are unable to land at the airport. In the terminal over 300 TopFlights passengers are becoming increasingly anxious – many have appointments to keep. We are then advised that Air Traffic Control has diverted the incoming aircraft to Leeds airport. So … three aircraft in Leeds and their corresponding passengers in Manchester. And my job? To sort it out!

Obviously this kind of **scenario** is unusual – but it can happen. As airport manager for northern England, I am responsible for overseeing all the TopFlights ground operations at both Manchester and Leeds airports. Essentially, this means that I look after all TopFlights activities at the airport, up until the point the aircraft takes off. This includes all aspects of passenger services (check-in, sales desks, departures and arrivals), as well as the behind-the-scenes operations such as baggage handling.

My time is divided between both airports, but as there are far more TopFlights flights to and from Manchester than Leeds (23 per day compared to five), the larger proportion of my time is spent at Manchester.

At both airports we work in close partnership with our handling agents, and a crucial part of my role is overseeing their practice to ensure that TopFlights passengers receive the very best service as they proceed through the airport and on to their flight. I organise regular training sessions and group activities with all our service staff.

Much of my job is about building strong relationships and partnerships, and I liaise closely with other airport managers to ensure that the interests of TopFlights are properly represented. TopFlights already has an established presence at Manchester (we are the third-largest airline there), but it lies with me to see that our profile remains high with the authorities, so that TopFlights continues to receive a good service.

Obviously safety is top of the agenda, and I am responsible for ensuring that we comply with all the standards and regulations set down by the relevant government bodies.

As a scheduled airline operating high-frequency, short-haul flights, another critical measure of our performance is the punctuality of our flights. As so many factors within the airport environment can affect punctuality, I continually **monitor** every aspect of our operation at both airports so that I can quickly identify areas of weakness and put measures in place to **rectify** these. Airports are complex environments and so, for everything to run smoothly, it's very important that everyone works as a team. Excellent communication skills are therefore essential. At times it can also be a stressful place, and so the ability to remain calm and maintain a sense of humour is also crucial! One of the things I really enjoy about my job is interacting with a wide variety of people – from passengers to airport senior management.

I keep fully up to date with what's going on at the airline by travelling down to the TopFlights offices at London Stansted airport regularly to meet with colleagues – including my **counterparts** from other TopFlights airports. We all share ideas and experiences so that we can continually improve the way in which we work. It's also my opportunity to give **feedback** about what's happening at my airports.

To succeed in this role you need to be adaptable and flexible, as no two days are ever the same and you have to deal with everything. It's not a job for people who like to **meticulously** plan out every minute of their day! But I really enjoy the pace and variety – and I can honestly say it's never boring.

19

## B Language and style

**2** The underlined words in Passage A have more than one meaning. Choose the one which is being used in this context.

| | | | |
|---|---|---|---|
| **a** corresponding: | letter-writing | matching | respective |
| **b** essentially: | necessarily | mainly | basically |
| **c** proportion: | size | ratio | part |
| **d** critical: | vital | finding fault | in a crisis |
| **e** deal: | trade | sort out | distribute |

**3** The following words from Passage A are useful but tricky to spell. Look at the bold 'hot-spot' (difficult part) in each word for a few seconds, then cover the word and try to write it correctly from memory.

Think of a rule or mnemonic (way of remembering) to help you remember the spelling of those words you find difficult.

**a** cru**cia**l _____

**b** re**cei**ve _____

**c** lia**i**se _____

**d** s**ch**eduled _____

**e** pu**nct**uality _____

**f** enviro**nm**ent _____

**g** ex**cell**ent _____

**h** coll**eague**s _____

**i** su**ccee**d _____

**j** **imme**diate _____

**4** Give synonyms for these words, which are in bold in Passage A:

**a** scenario _____

**b** monitor _____

**c** rectify _____

**d** counterparts _____

**e** feedback _____

**f** meticulously _____

**5** Put as many prefixes as possible on to the following stems.

For example: -prove   improve, approve, reprove, disprove

**a** -vert _____

**b** -port _____

**c** -sult _____

**d** -sent _____

**e** -ply _____

**6**  Write a sentence containing each word below to show the difference in meaning between the words in each pair.

**a**  proceed _____

   precede _____

**b**  lie _____

   lay _____

**c**  affect _____

   effect _____

**d**  continuous _____

   continual _____

**e**  principal _____

   principle _____

**f**  whose _____

   who's _____

**g**  uninterested _____

   disinterested _____

**7**  Circle the single dashes and hyphens used in the text. First work out the rules for their usage and then give other examples of your own.

**a**  Dashes have a space either side and are used singly to:_____

   _____

   For example: _____

   _____

   _____

**b**  Hyphens, which do not have spaces before or after, are used to: _____

   _____

   For example: _____

   _____

   _____

**8** **a** Who do you think is the audience for Passage **A**?

_____

_____

_____

**b** List the features of the passage that are typical of spoken informal language.

_____

_____

_____

_____

_____

_____

_____

_____

## C Comprehension and summary

**9** In a paragraph, give the facts about the airline in Passage **A**.

_____

_____

_____

_____

_____

_____

_____

_____

_____

_____

_____

_____

_____

_____

_____

_____

_____

**10** In a paragraph, describe the qualities needed for the job of airport manager.

_____

_____

_____

_____

_____

_____

_____

_____

_____

_____

_____

_____

_____

_____

_____

_____

**11** In a paragraph, summarise the responsibilities and tasks of an airport manager.

_____

_____

_____

_____

_____

_____

_____

_____

_____

_____

_____

_____

_____

_____

## D Reading

**12  Read the article below.**

### Passage B: Junior jet set

An estimated 7 million children a year travel alone by air, many as young as seven. Some are travelling between home and their boarding schools in the UK, particularly from Asia. Last year, one airline alone carried 3000 flyers aged between five and 11. Specialist staff are provided by airlines, known in the trade as 'aunties', to escort these transcontinental commuters from check-in to aircraft. They have to reassure nervous flyers and give them cuddles, and even clean clothes if necessary.

The children tend to be treated as VIPs, being seated and fed before the other passengers. They pass the time with video games and puzzles, and are so well looked after that many say they prefer flying solo to travelling with their families!

At the other end, the 'unmins' or 'ums' as they are nicknamed (standing for 'unaccompanied minors') are collected from the plane and delivered to the designated adult meeting the child.

Some US airlines charge for this service, but most European and Asian ones do not. Teenagers up to 16 or 17 – depending on the airline – are called 'young passengers' and are still accompanied to the pick-up.

Things rarely go wrong, but it has been known for a child to be flown to the wrong destination, and cancelled connecting flights can create the headache of having to put up the stranded youngster in a hotel.

## E Comprehension and summary

**13  Read the tips below.**

### Tips for the parents of 'unmins'

a  Train your child to recite their name, address and phone number.

b  Give your child some money.

c  Take novice flyers on a tour of the airport before the day they fly.

d  Arrange for them to travel at off-peak times.

e  Avoid night flights.

f  Don't leave the airport until you have seen the plane take off.

g  Book an aisle seat.

h  Ask for your child to be seated near other children.

**14** Infer the reason for each tip in the box at the foot of page 25.

a _____

b _____

c _____

d _____

e _____

f _____

g _____

h _____

**15** Using information and ideas from Passages **A** and **B**, write a dialogue between a child flyer and the airport manager, who has been called by an 'auntie' to settle an anxiety or problem the child is having.

**AM:** Hello. My name is Sue Watson and I'm the airport manager here. What can I do to help?

**Child:** _____

_____

_____

_____

_____

_____

_____

_____

_____

_____

_____

_____

_____

_____

_____

_____

## F Directed writing

**16** Read the recruitment advertisement below.

# WANT TO WORK FOR US?

**Looking for a new challenge with an interesting and dynamic company? Take a look at these exciting career opportunities at TopFlights …**

## Come fly with us …

We are currently recruiting Cabin Crew for our base at London Stansted.

Our Cabin Crew must ensure that our customers' safety and comfort come first and that they create a memorable experience by providing friendly and courteous service at all times. The job is busy and can be physically demanding. Cabin Crew have to be prepared to work on any day of the year, any time of the day.

**You must be:**

- friendly and approachable
- mature in attitude and behaviour
- able to remain calm and efficient under pressure
- an excellent communicator with people of all ages and cultures
- a team player
- flexible and adaptable
- able to take the initiative
- willing to accept guidance.

**Minimum requirements:**

- age 20+
- height 1.58 m to 1.82 m with weight in proportion to height
- physically fit and able to pass a medical assessment
- fluent in English, both spoken and written
- good standard in at least one other language
- able to swim 25 m
- possess a passport allowing unrestricted travel within Europe.

If you meet all of our person specifications and minimum requirements,
please request an application form from:

Cabin Crew Applications

TopFlights Airline Company Ltd

London Stansted Airport

Essex, UK

27

17  Write a job application letter to the personnel manager of TopFlights, saying why the job would suit you and why you would suit the job. You may also add any extra material of your own that you consider relevant.

## G Composition

### Descriptive writing

a   Describe the atmosphere of a busy airport, referring to particular people and situations that you observe.

b   Describe, in role, an hour in the day of a flight attendant, including your thoughts and feelings during that time.

### Narrative writing

c   Write a story that involves a farewell scene.

d   'An unforgettable plane journey'. Write a story with this title.

1   'My experiences and views of travelling by air, and how I think air travel might change during my lifetime'.

2   Write a story about a major incident that occurred on a plane or in an airport.

*Coursework topics*

# Unit 4: On the ball

## A Reading

**1 Read the article below.**

### Passage A: Love it or hate it

In viewing terms, the World Cup is twice as big as any other sporting event on the planet. But just because it's big doesn't mean it's beautiful; football can bring out the worst in people, particularly men: it can make them obsessive and boring; it can make them prejudiced and intolerant; it can make them violent and destructive. But despite the corruption and cynicism surrounding it, football has never lost its appeal.

Football weaves itself into whichever cultures embrace it, appealing to people who have nothing else in common but who each have a personal passion for the game and are addicted to its spontaneity. Packaged into 90 minutes are heroes and villains, hope and despair, skill and drama: a miniature war with flags and armies.

Football has an astonishing ability to cross borders and barriers, as between German and British troops in no-man's-land in the First World War. It seems so natural to share the kicking of a ball, and the basic structure of the game is amazingly simple: two opposing sides attempt to push a spherical object into the other's goal. Played informally, football has great flexibility, with no set number of players, no particular pitch and no equipment except something to kick and something to define the goal mouth.

Anthropologists have explained men's universal and enduring fascination with football as being a replacement and compensation for the hunter-gatherer instincts which have no outlet in the 21st century. It is a substitute for the hunt, combining the necessary elements of a group of males, adrenalin and the prospect of reward. Many ancient civilisations – China, Japan, Greece and Rome – all had equivalents of the game, which they exported, as did the British, to parts of their far-flung empires.

Documentary evidence dates football back to 1175 in England, when Shrove Tuesday, immediately before the beginning of Lent and abstinence, was the big day in the footballing calendar. During the 1830s, matches were becoming nothing better than a series of punch-ups, so they were stamped out briefly. By 1863 the Football Association had been set up in London between 11 clubs after a meeting at Cambridge University to agree a set of rules. The people who attended the meeting were PE teachers from famous public schools and 'old boys' who had continued to play the game after leaving school. By the 1870s, the game had become professional, and international fixtures were being arranged with countries in South America and northern Europe. This is the origin of the modern World Cup, following the evolution of FIFA as an international football organisation, and live radio coverage, which became possible in 1927.

No other single sport has brought together nations and individuals so much or provided more pleasure over a longer period of time. Football has also, however, given the world things it would be much better without: riots, vandalism, hooliganism and tribalism. More recently, it's become a vehicle for an upsurge in nationalism, racism and fascism, the full consequences of which are still fearfully awaited. It's been taken over by the mass media; huge sums of money are involved in advertising, sponsorship, transfer fees, merchandise and broadcasting rights. It's turned into soap opera, with players (and their wives and girlfriends) treated as idols and celebrities – rather than mere mortals with skilful feet – and deprived of a private life.

## B Language and style

2  **a**  Circle the apostrophes (') in Passage A. Explain the two usages of apostrophes.

We use apostrophes either when we _____

(for example: _____)

or when we _____

(for example: _____).

An apostrophe after the final **s** of a word, unless it is a name, indicates that _____

_____

(for example: _____).

**b**  In the passage there are examples of *it's* with an apostrophe and *its* without an apostrophe. What is the difference?

We use an apostrophe in *it's* if _____

_____

whereas *its* without an apostrophe is used to _____

_____.

3  **Circle the semicolons (;) in Passage A and define their usage by filling the gaps below.**

Semicolons, which are used sparingly and only for a good reason, have the same function as

_____ ; but are used when the preceding sentence has a _____

with the following sentence. They can also be used to separate _____ .

4  **Underline the 'hot-spots' in the following words from Passage A. Look up the meaning of any words you are not sure of. Cover them up, then practise writing them correctly.**

**a**  beautiful _____

**b**  cynicism _____

**c**  spontaneity _____

**d**  villains _____

**e**  miniature _____

**f**  attempt _____

**g**  calendar _____

**h** professional _____

**i** vehicle _____

**j** skilful _____

## C Comprehension and summary

5 Highlight the relevant points in Passage **A** and write a chronological summary of the history of football, using your own words as far as possible.

_____

_____

_____

_____

_____

_____

_____

_____

_____

_____

_____

_____

_____

_____

_____

_____

_____

_____

_____

_____

## D Directed writing

6   Write a letter to the author of Passage **A**, responding to the their views on football and saying whether or not you think they are fair.

_____

_____

_____

_____

_____

_____

_____

_____

_____

_____

_____

_____

_____

_____

_____

_____

_____

_____

_____

_____

## E Reading

**7** **Read the article below.**

### Passage B: Really royal

There has been a recent rise in interest in the game of real tennis, the ancestor of modern tennis and also the forerunner of squash, rackets and badminton. Although it is still a niche sport that has only 10,000 players in four countries – France, Britain, Australia and the USA – it is now on the up for the first time since the First World War started in 1914.

'Real' is a corruption of the word 'royal', and real tennis goes back to the shape of the court and the rules of tennis in medieval times, when it was a game played by kings, notably the French and English monarchs. When it was brought to England from France in the 1530s, Henry VIII was a keen player, despite his not inconsiderable bulk.

Modern lawn tennis is played outdoors on symmetrical and parallel-lined grass or clay courts, using fluorescent yellow balls and graphite racquets – although until comparatively recently the balls were white and the racquets were wooden and heavy. In the Middle Ages, tennis was an indoor game and the courts were not only huge – the size of banqueting halls – but also asymmetrical. Real tennis is a cross between tennis and squash; it is still played on an indoor court, one which has high black walls and a buttress or 'tambour', that is a sloping roof – but only on one side – against which every serve must bounce. The spectators watch from a viewing gallery or 'penthouse'. The other end of the court is open and is referred to as the 'dedans'. The balls are solid, and therefore heavy. Even stranger, every court is different in size, although they all have the same markings. These are important because they enable the return of the ball even when normal rules of tennis are broken, such as the ball bouncing more than once. This makes the game less demanding in some ways than modern tennis, and attractive to older and less fit players – as well as total beginners – because they can still win points without having to run around too much.

An Australian club coach has this to say about this increasingly popular game, which now even makes it into the sports news from time to time: 'The rules and scoring system admittedly seem bizarre at first and take a bit of getting used to, but the fun of it is that it's a uniquely three-dimensional game. The ball comes at you from all angles, and there are lots of different options of how to play it. You have to become proficient at various types of shot, but mostly it's a question of learning how to read the game and use tactical skills, just like in chess. Most real tennis clubs are encouraging to potential players who phone up and say "I've heard or read about this game called real tennis. Can you tell me more about it? I'd love to give it a go!"'

## F Language and style

**8** **Draw lines to match the following words from Passage B to their meanings in the second column.**

a   niche                   strategic

b   corruption              specialised

c   asymmetrical            accomplished

d   proficient              debasement

e   tactical                lopsided

9   Look at the way direct speech is punctuated in Passage **B**. Fill in the gaps below to remind yourself of the rules for punctuating speech.

Within speech, most of the same punctuation rules apply as for normal writing, so that there

needs to be a _____ at the end of a sentence, provided that there is no

continuation of the sentence after the end of the speech. If there is, then in place of the full stop we

use a _____ or, if appropriate, a question mark or exclamation mark can be used.

Even after a question or exclamation mark, the next word begins with a _____

letter rather than a _____ if it is continuing the sentence. If a sentence in speech

is interrupted and then continued, there is a _____ before the break and again

before the re-opening of the inverted commas. The continuation will begin with a small letter

and not a capital because the _____ is also continuing. There must always

be a punctuation mark of some kind before the closing _____ .

If a speech contains speech or quotation, then the inner speech must use the opposite kind of

_____ from the outer speech, whether single or double.

10   Look at the following words from Passage **B** and formulate a spelling rule for double letters. Give other similar examples.

   **gallery      different      attractive      tennis      admittedly**

   Rule: _____

   _____

   _____

   Examples: _____

   _____

11   Look at the following words from Passage **B**. Work out the meanings of the prefixes, then use them to make other words.

   **fore(runner)      medi(eval)      sym(metrical)      para(llel)      en(couraging)**

   Meanings: _____

   _____

   _____

   Other words: _____

   _____

**12** Passage **B** contains some idiomatic expressions. Use the following phrases in sentences of your own to show their meaning.

**a** on the up _____

_____

**b** not inconsiderable _____

_____

**c** a cross between _____

_____

**d** from time to time _____

_____

**e** give it a go _____

_____

**13** The following words from Passage **B** are difficult to spell. Use the Look, Cover, Write, Check method to learn them, then write them out again.

ancestor _____

fluorescent _____

racquet _____

bizarre _____

uniquely _____

# G Comprehension and summary

**14** Using information from Passage **B**, write two paragraphs of not more than 75 words each about real tennis: **a** the historical background of the game; **b** the unusual features of the game.

**a** _____

_____

_____

_____

_____

_____

_____

_____

_____

_____

_____

**b** _____

_____

_____

_____

_____

_____

_____

## H Directed writing

**15** Imagine you are a club coach answering a phone call from someone interested in taking up real tennis. Write a sequence of five questions and answers to use as much as possible of the relevant material in Passage **B**.

**Caller:** I've heard about this game called real tennis. Can you tell me something about it?

**Coach:** _____

_____

_____

_____

_____

_____

_____

_____

_____

_____

_____

_____

_____

_____

_____

_____

_____

_____

_____

_____

_____

## I Composition

### Descriptive writing

a  Describe the experience of being in a large and uncontrolled crowd.

b  Describe the climactic minutes in a competition between two players.

### Narrative writing

c  Write a story about a group of sports fans.

d  Write a story about someone who achieves 'fifteen minutes of fame'.

1  'It matters not who won or lost, but how you played the game.' Discuss the meaning of this line of poetry and whether this view is still appropriate in today's world.

2  Write a descriptive or narrative piece entitled 'The match'.

Coursework topics

# Unit 5: Great rivers

## A Reading

**1    Read the article below.**

### Passage A: Amazon facts

What makes the Amazon the greatest river in the world is the volume of water that it carries; it **produces** 20% of the world's river water. Although the Nile river in Africa is the longest river in the world (at 6650 km long to the Amazon's approximate 6280 km), the Nile does not carry a 60th of the amount of water that the Amazon does, because the latter river drains the entire northern half of the South American continent. The torrential tropical rains deluge the rainforests with over 10 metres a year, and rainfall in the region is a near daily **occurrence**. The Amazon is also the world's widest river (6–10 km), and the mouth of the Amazon, where it meets the sea, is so **deep** as well as wide that ocean-going ships have navigated its waters far inland. It becomes even wider when it floods in the wet season.

The precise source of the Amazon was only recently discovered, although the **origins** of most of the Earth's great rivers have been known for some time, and the quest to find the Amazon's origin in the most inaccessible part of the world had intrigued **explorers** for centuries. Determining the source of the Amazon has been so difficult because of a combination of unfriendly terrain, high altitudes, cold winds and the large number of potential headwater streams that needed to be investigated. What defines a river's origin is the most distant point from the mouth (as **measured** along the river's course and not by the way the crow flies) from which water flows year round along the main trunk of the river, not including the tributaries.

In 2001, a 22-member international team of mappers and explorers, **sponsored** by the National Geographic Society, claimed to have pin-pointed the source of the Amazon river. The team explored five different headwater streams in the Andes before they were **convinced** that they had **definitely** discovered the place where drops of water first collect to form the mighty Amazon. According to the team, the Amazon's origin is a small mountain stream that flows from the sides of Nevado Mismi, a 5600-metre mountain in southern Peru. A global positioning system (GPS), linked to a network of satellites, was employed to precisely locate the source, which is less than 160 km from the Pacific Ocean.

Famously, the Amazon river is home to many exotic and **extreme** tropical creatures, such as catfish, anaconda (biggest snake) and piranha (most ferocious fish), as well as the macaws and tapirs that add their colours and sounds to the jungle.

## B Language and style

2   Fill in the table below with the missing part(s) of speech that go with the word given (e.g. a suitable noun for 'produces' is 'product'). Each word is one of the words in bold in Passage A. In some cases you may be able to find more than one word that fits the part of speech, and in others none.

| Noun | Adjective | Verb | Adverb |
|---|---|---|---|
|  |  | produces |  |
| occurrence |  |  |  |
|  | deep |  |  |
| origins |  |  |  |
| explorers |  |  |  |
|  |  | measured |  |
|  |  | sponsored |  |
|  |  | convinced |  |
|  |  |  | definitely |
|  | extreme |  |  |

3   Circle all the commas in Passage A and study how they are used. Work out and define the five ways in which commas are used, giving an example of each.

a _____

_____

For example: _____

b _____

_____

For example: _____

c _____

_____

For example: _____

d _____

_____

For example: _____

e _____

_____

For example: _____

4 **a** Complex sentences are constructed by linking subordinate clauses to a main clause using connectives, and by adding participle phrases (present or past, with or without a preposition). Underline examples of different types of linking in Passage **A**.

   **b** Link the three simple sentences below into **one complex sentence** in as many ways as you can. You may need to make changes to the grammar or word order. (Note that *and, but, so* and *or* form **compound** and not complex sentences.)

   **i** The source of the Amazon has only recently been discovered.

   **ii** The source is located 160 km from the Pacific Ocean.

   **iii** Explorers tried for centuries to discover the river's source.

   _____

   _____

   _____

   _____

   _____

   _____

   _____

   _____

   _____

   _____

## C Comprehension and summary

5 **In two sentences, using connectives and participles, summarise the information in the first paragraph of Passage A.**

   _____

   _____

   _____

   _____

   _____

   _____

   _____

   _____

# D Reading

**6** Read the article below.

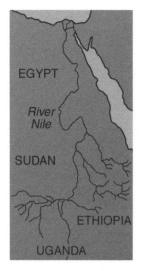

## Passage B: Life and death on the Nile

For Egyptians, farmers and fishermen, the Nile is not just a beautiful view, it is a gift, without which there could be no Egypt, only a scorched wasteland. In a country that does not receive much rainfall, the river is their livelihood. It covers only 4% of the country but its banks are where almost all of the 67 million Egyptians live. The Nile irrigates corn crops and citrus orchards, and provides water for herds of cows and for doing the laundry. Its seasons are the rhythms of the Egyptian way of life; when it floods every July, locals move to higher ground until it subsides three months later.

The waters of the Nile flow for nearly 7000 km, from the jungles of Uganda through the deserts of Sudan to arrive at Cairo, Africa's largest city. For centuries no-one knew where it began, and the whereabouts of its source was a legend and a quest – a dangerous one, as the Nile contains crocodiles and intruders into the heart of Africa were often not welcomed by the natives. The source was finally discovered in the mid-19th century.

The world's longest river is a personality in myth as well as in reality. It features in many memorable scenes in the Bible and in literature, ancient and modern. It was assigned to the god Isis, to be honoured with offerings of food, and it was believed that the pharaohs could control it through their magical powers. The pyramids could not have been built without the means of transport provided by the great river.

Local stories tell of mythical creatures, some half-human and half-fish, which inhabit the river and sometimes take a fancy to humans and take them to live at the bottom; and of others which own the river and must be fed and kept happy or they will cause harm. The Egyptian queen Cleopatra was nicknamed the Serpent of Old Nile, and it was believed that the river mud had creative powers and produced snakes. Many films and books have used the romantic and threatening setting of the river, including the famous Agatha Christie detective novel *Death on the Nile*.

Since the advent of cruise liners and the influx of tourists, however, life on the riverbank has changed, and Egyptians say that the Nile is no longer theirs. Although it is, in fact, chemical fertilisers that are largely responsible, local opinion is that the leisure boats have polluted the water. They watch as the great city of Cairo continues to spread its garish hotels and grey apartment blocks along the banks in a ribbon development that shows no signs of stopping.

# E Language and style

**7** Read the extract below from Joseph Conrad's *Heart of Darkness*.

Going up that river was like travelling back to the earliest beginnings of the world, when vegetation rioted on the earth and the big trees were kings. An empty stream, a great silence, an impenetrable forest. The air was warm, thick, heavy, sluggish. There was no joy in the brilliance of sunshine. The long stretches of the waterway ran on, deserted, into the gloom of overshadowed distances. On silvery sandbanks hippos and alligators sunned themselves side by side. The broadening waters flowed through a mob of wooded islands; you lost your way on that river as you would in a desert, and butted all day long against shoals, trying to find the channel, till you thought yourself bewitched and cut off for ever from everything you had known once – somewhere – far away – in another existence perhaps. There were moments when one's past came back to one, as it will sometimes when you have not a moment to spare to yourself; but it came in the shape of an unrestful and noisy dream, remembered with wonder amongst the overwhelming realities of this strange world of plants, and water, and silence. And this stillness of life did not in the least resemble a peace. It was the stillness of an implacable force brooding over an inscrutable intention. It looked at you with a vengeful aspect.

**8** The extract describes the River Congo. Choose five words or phrases that convey the feeling of:

**a** mystery _____

_____

**b** threat _____

_____

**9** In what ways does the description of the river in the extract above differ from the descriptions of the rivers in Passages **A** and **B**? Look at the difference in vocabulary and its effects.

_____

_____

_____

_____

_____

_____

_____

_____

_____

_____

_____

_____

_____

_____

_____

_____

_____

_____

_____

_____

## F Comprehension and summary

**10** List the facts and the fictions about the River Nile from Passage **B**.

Facts

Fictions

_____ _____

_____ _____

_____ _____

_____ _____

_____ _____

_____ _____

_____ _____

_____ _____

_____ _____

**11** List the similarities and differences between the Nile and the Amazon from Passages **A** and **B**.

Similarities

Differences

_____ _____

_____ _____

_____ _____

_____ _____

_____ _____

_____ _____

_____ _____

_____ _____

_____ _____

## G Directed writing

12 Imagine you have just returned from a cruise on the River Nile. Write a letter to your travel agent to complain that you were disappointed because it did not live up to your expectations. Use information and ideas from Passage B in your letter.

_____

_____

_____

_____

_____

_____

_____

_____

_____

_____

_____

_____

_____

_____

_____

_____

_____

_____

_____

_____

_____

_____

_____

_____

_____

_____

_____

_____

_____

_____

_____

_____

_____

_____

_____

## H Composition

### Descriptive writing

a   Describe a harbour.

b   Think of a place you have always wanted to visit. Describe how you see it in your imagination.

### Narrative writing

c   'The quest'. Write a story with this title.

d   'Towards evening, they finally arrived at their destination, but it was not at all what they had been expecting.' Continue this story.

1   'Travel broadens the mind.' Argue for or against this claim, in the context of contemporary mass tourism.

2   Write a story that ends with 'And the ship sailed on.'

Coursework topics

# Unit 6: Trunk tales

## A Reading

**1    Read the article below.**

### Passage A: The artistic elephant

An elephant called Noppakhao, also known as Peter, has painted dozens of works over the last few years, some of them **fetching** as much as $700. He has a delicate brushstroke, a deliberate and <u>controlled</u> style, and an eye for colour that would give Picasso a run for his money. He paints pictures of other elephants, landscapes and flowers, <u>preferring</u> to paint from life rather than to <u>produce</u> abstract works. His most recent painting is a self-portrait.

Noppakhao – whose name <u>translates</u> as 'nine colours of the gemstones' – lives in Ayutthaya province in Thailand. He was <u>introduced</u> to painting eight years ago as part of the Asian Elephant Art & Conservation Project, and the purpose of his artistic **endeavours** is to raise money for his **keep** and that of the 90 other elephants on the site, as well as for the training of caretakers. He works with his *mahout*, Mr Pipat Salamgam.

He is a popular and <u>extrovert</u> elephant who loves fun and being the centre of attention. According to his keepers, the 11-year-old bull elephant <u>exhibits</u> a wonderful sense of **dexterity** with the paintbrush. His *mahout* <u>replenishes</u> his brush with paint, but all the movements he makes with it grasped in his trunk are his own. The 'canvas' is paper produced from elephant dung, which is beautifully textured, odourless, and environmentally **sound**.

In the past, elephant painting has led to accusations that the animals are harshly treated in efforts to train them. However, the AEACP insists it does not **tolerate** any abuse of the elephants, either while painting or in everyday <u>interaction</u>. It says: 'We **strive** to give as many elephants as we can a happy, healthy, <u>enriched</u> existence. Money raised by the AEACP is used to provide **captive** elephants with better food, improved shelter and proper veterinary care.'

## B Language and style

2 Find replacement words for the following, in the context in which they are used in Passage **A**.

a fetching _____     e sound _____

b endeavours _____     f tolerate _____

c keep _____     g strive _____

d dexterity _____     h captive _____

3 Judging from the examples in underlined words in the passage, what do the following prefixes mean? Give two more examples of words beginning with each prefix.

a con-_____

b pre-_____

c pro-_____

d trans-_____

e intr-_____

f extr-_____

g ex-_____

h re-_____

i inter-_____

j en-_____

4 What is the number associated with the following words? Look up those which you don't know.

a thrice _____     i dozen _____

b duet _____     j score _____

c December _____     k fortnight _____

d hexagonal _____     l trinity _____

e pentagon _____     m September _____

f binary _____     n monopoly _____

g universal _____     o gross _____

h quadruple _____

## C Comprehension and summary

5   Select the facts from Passage **A** that are relevant, put them into a suitable order, then write a
    news report with the headline 'Elephant Picasso paints self-portrait!'

_____

_____

_____

_____

_____

_____

_____

_____

_____

_____

_____

_____

_____

_____

_____

_____

_____

_____

_____

_____

# D Directed writing

6   Imagine that you have visited the Asian Elephant Art & Conservation project and watched the elephant painting. Using and developing information from Passage A, write a letter or email to a friend or member of the family telling them, in your own words, about your experience.

_____

_____

_____

_____

_____

_____

_____

_____

_____

_____

_____

_____

_____

_____

_____

_____

_____

_____

_____

## E Reading

**7    Read the story below.**

## Passage B: The Elephant and the Blind Men

Once upon a time, in a faraway land, there lived six blind men. They were friends, but each of them thought himself very wise, much wiser than the others.

One day these six wise blind men went for a walk in a zoo. They could not see the animals but they wanted to listen to them, and they were especially interested in the elephant, of which they had heard much.

That day the zoo-keeper had forgotten to lock the gate of the elephant's cage. Elephants are naturally very curious animals, so it immediately pushed the gate to the cage to see if it might open. To its great delight, it swung wide and the elephant was able to stroll through. Just at that moment the six blind men were passing the elephant's cage. One of them heard a twig snap and went over to see what it was that was walking nearby.

'Greetings!' said the first blind man to the elephant. 'Could you please tell us the way to the elephant enclosure?' The elephant made no noise, but it shifted its weight from left to right, and rocked backwards and forwards. The first blind man walked over to see if this big silent person needed any help. With a bump, he walked right into the side of the elephant. He put out his arms to either side, but all he could feel was the unyielding body of the elephant stretching away in both directions. The first blind man said to the others, 'I think I must have walked into a wall. That's the only explanation.'

The second blind man joined the first. He took up a position to the front of the elephant and grabbed hold of the animal's trunk. He quickly let go of it and shouted, 'Don't be ridiculous. This isn't a wall. This is a snake! We should keep away in case it's poisonous.'

The third man didn't believe either of the other two and decided to find out for himself what it was. He walked to the rear of the elephant and touched its tail. He laughed and said, 'This is neither a wall or a snake. You are both wrong once again. It is quite clear that this is a rope.'

The fourth man knew how opinionated and stubborn his friends could be, always claiming that they were right and the others wrong. He took it upon himself to give his verdict and settle the matter. He crouched down and felt around the bottom of one of the elephant's legs. 'My dear friends,' explained the fourth man, 'this is neither a wall nor a snake. It is no rope either. What we have here, gentlemen, is a tree trunk. That's all there is to say. Let's move on.'

The fifth man had become impatient by now and he realised that it was up to him to pronounce definitively upon the matter. He walked up to the front side of the elephant and felt one of the animal's long tusks. 'What I am holding is long and curved and sharp at the end. It must be a spear. It is not safe to stay here.'

The sixth blind man was by now very puzzled that so many and such different answers could have been given by his five friends. He walked up to the front side of the elephant and grabbed something huge which flapped. He dismissed the other explanations and stated categorically that what they had found was a fan.

The six erstwhile friends began arguing with each other, each maintaining that they alone were right and justifying their opinion. They became very aggressive about it, and started insulting each other.

The zoo-keeper heard the noise the men were making, ran to where they were, and took hold of the escaped elephant, speaking gently to it. The sixth blind man called out, 'Could you please help us? My friends and I do not seem able to figure out what this nearby object is. One of us thinks it's a wall; one thinks it's a snake; one thinks it's a rope; one thinks it's four tree trunks; one thinks it's a sharp weapon. We are in danger of seriously falling out about this matter. Which of us is right, and how can one thing seem so different to six people?'

'Well,' said the zoo-keeper, 'you are all right. And you are all wrong. This is an elephant, but because you each encountered only a part of it, none of you were able to recognise what it really is.'

## F Language and style

**8** **Without looking at Passage B again until you have finished the exercise, write out the following extract from it with all the necessary punctuation added.**

my dear friends explained the fourth man this is neither a wall nor a snake it is no rope either what we have here gentlemen is four tree trunks thats all there is to say lets move on

_____

_____

_____

_____

## G Comprehension and summary

**9** **a** Write the moral of the story, using your own words.

_____

_____

_____

_____

**b** Rewrite the story in a shorter version, using not more than 200 words (Passage **B** is 762 words).

_____

_____

_____

_____

_____

_____

_____

_____

_____

_____

_____

_____

_____

_____

_____

_____

_____

_____

_____

## H Composition

### Descriptive writing

**a** Describe an animal you have seen in its natural habitat, giving details of its appearance and its behaviour at that time.

**b** Describe the experience of seeing a person or an animal performing an extraordinary feat.

### Narrative writing

**c** Write a story that is set in a zoo.

**d** Write a story in which the main character is blind.

**1** Discuss the role played by various animals in different cultures and the human attitudes towards them.

**2** Describe a visit to a circus, including the atmosphere and some of the spectators.

Coursework topics

# Unit 7: Bricks and stones

## A Reading

**1    Read the article below.**

### Passage A: Lost marbles

For 200 years there has been a bitter argument between Greece and Britain over the ownership of the Elgin marbles. The issue raises high passions and poses difficult political, legal, moral and cultural questions with far-reaching implications. Although nearly half of the Britons **polled** had no opinion on the matter, 40% of the other half were in favour of returning the marbles to Greece. Greeks are, of course, **unanimous** in their demand.

Dedicated to the goddess Athena, protector of Athens, the marble panels adorning the sacred temple of the Parthenon were removed in August 1801 under the orders of the Earl of Elgin, British Ambassador to the Ottoman Empire, who was a keen collector of antiquities. He intended to use them to decorate his stately home in Scotland. In 1816, they were bought by the British Museum in London. The frieze dates from the time of Pericles, who was the ruler of Athens in the 5th century BCE during its golden age of democracy, philosophy and the arts, a period which was of **profound** and lasting importance for the civilisation of Europe. The carvings show scenes of struggle between men, gods, centaurs and giants, echoing recent battles. They were sculpted by Phidias, who is regarded as the greatest artist of the ancient world.

Much damage was caused to the temple by the removal of the *metopes* (carved panels), when they began a **perilous** journey which took some of the marbles to the bottom of the sea. One shipload of marbles on board a British ship which was travelling to Scotland was caught in a storm and sank near the Greek island of Kythera. It took two years to salvage the marbles and bring them to the surface.

Since the alleged original document of sale has not been located, no-one knows whether Lord Elgin had paid for them in the first place, except for the necessary bribes and site licences; certainly he does not seem to have had permission to remove sculptures still attached to the temple. Lord Byron, who strongly objected to their removal from Greece, **denounced** Elgin as a vandal.

Another of his contemporaries, the Romantic poet John Keats, saw them exhibited in London and he was inspired to write two sonnets about them.

Those in favour of the return of the marbles believe they should be reunited with other Greek sculptures in sight of the building that they once adorned, a move for which there is worldwide public support.

The Greeks, who have been seeking the return of the marbles since 1829, when their country became independent, view them as an **intrinsic** part of their national identity and culture, as the essence of Greekness. They have offered various guarantees for the return of their treasures: providing a temperature-controlled, world-class museum to house and display them; paying the cost of their transport to Athens; donating other pieces in a reciprocal exchange; and accepting them as a long-term loan, without transference of ownership. Fragments of the marbles have already been returned by other countries, including the USA. Supporters also point out that Aboriginal ancestral human remains were returned to Tasmania after a 20-year battle with Australia, despite the existence of the British Museum charter preventing the repatriation of items in its collection.

Those who resist the demand for the restitution of the marbles point out that they would not have survived at all had they remained in Athens, and that Lord Elgin saved them for **posterity**. The city fell to Byzantines, Franks and Turks, and the Parthenon was damaged by fire and earthquake as recently as 1981. In 1687, during a siege, the Turkish garrison's gunpowder stored inside the Parthenon was ignited, bringing down walls and columns, and the Acropolis was twice besieged during the Greek War of Independence in the 1820s. The Venetians shattered the horses of Athena and Poseidon while they were trying to remove them, and other pieces had been carried off to the Louvre museum in Paris before Elgin's 'theft' and relocation of the marbles in 1801.

However, while the artefacts held in London may have been saved from the hazards of war, they suffered gravely from 19th-century pollution and were **irrevocably** damaged by cleaning methods employed by British Museum staff, which destroyed the original fine detail of the carving.

The British Museum continues to resist political pressure and intends to hold on to its prize exhibits. Officials claim that the return of the marbles to Greece would open the floodgates to all countries wanting their antiquities back, and the world's museums and libraries would have to **dismantle** their collections and close down, thereby **diminishing** their own nation's educational and financial resources. Tourist attractions would be rendered national rather than international, which, they argue, would be a retrograde step, as links and comparisons between the world's greatest artefacts can only be possible

*frieze*: a decorated horizontal band along the upper part of a wall

in international exhibitions. Since more than half the original marbles are lost, the return of the ones in Britain would not complete the collection.

The Museum takes the view that history cannot be rewound and that by displaying the marbles in London – and by not charging for entry – the Museum has spread the culture of classical Greek civilisation, which has been an inspiration to generations of people of all nationalities.

55

# B  Language and style

**2**  **Give single words or phrases as synonyms for the following words from Passage A.**

**a**  polled _____

**b**  unanimous _____

**c**  profound _____

**d**  perilous _____

**e**  denounced _____

**f**  intrinsic _____

**g**  posterity _____

**h**  irrevocably _____

**i**  dismantle _____

**j**  diminishing _____

**3** Underline all the words beginning with *re* in Passage **A**. Write down those which are the correct synonyms for the following words or phrases.

**a** joined again _____     **f** turned back _____

**b** taken away _____     **g** change of place _____

**c** in return _____     **h** return to country of origin _____

**d** oppose _____     **i** moving backwards _____

**e** return to owner _____     **j** supplies _____

**4** Using different colours for each tense, underline or highlight in Passage **A** all the verbs in the four past tenses: present perfect, simple past, past continuous, past perfect. Fill in the gaps below to explain their usage.

For a completed and dated action in the past we use the _____ ,

whereas for an action which began in the past but which is not yet completed we use the _____

_____ . The past perfect tense is used when an action _____

_____ . The past continuous shows that

an action when _____ .

**5** Circle all the uses of *which* and *who* in Passage **A**. Notice that when followed by a comma, they are adding separate information about the noun; when there is no comma, they are part of the definition of the noun. Join the simple sentences below into one complex sentence by using *which* or *who*, and a comma if necessary.

**a** I visited the exhibition. I heard about it on the radio.

_____

**b** I read about the man. He had stolen the statues.

_____

**c** I bought a book. It was about the history of Greece.

_____

**d** I met Lord Byron. He had written a poem the previous day.

_____

**e** We have not visited Greece. We have heard it is a beautiful country.

_____

**f** I spoke to a woman in the gallery. She was the one I had met previously.

_____

**g** It is difficult to find the people. They are responsible for the damage.

_____

**h** This is the Museum Director. He is against the return of the marbles.

_____

**i** They didn't find the sculpture. It was buried by an earthquake.

_____

**j** You should have interviewed Lord Elgin. I introduced him to you.

_____

## C Comprehension and summary

**6** **a** What percentage of Greeks want the marbles returned to Greece?

_____

**b** How did some of the marbles end up on the sea bed?

_____

**c** Who had a 20-year battle with Australia?

_____

**d** What caused damage to the marbles?

_____

**e** What were the responses by Elgin's contemporaries to the marbles being displayed in London?

_____

**7** **Use the information in Passage A to write a dialogue between a British Museum official and a representative of the Greek Ministry of Culture, who argue about who should have custody of the Elgin marbles.**

**MC:** I must insist on behalf of the Greek people that this important part of our cultural heritage is returned to where it belongs.

**BM:** _____

_____

_____

_____

_____

## D Directed writing

8   Write a letter to the editor of a national newspaper, giving your view on whether artefacts such as the Elgin Marbles should be returned to their country of origin or kept in museums in other countries.

## E Reading

**9  Read the article below.**

## Passage B: High water

Every winter Venice fears the *acqua alta*, which threatens to **overwhelm** it; **relentless** high tides are eating into the wooden doors and shutters of ground-floor apartments. No-one lives on the ground floor any more and Venetians are leaving their drowning home; the population has **dwindled** by 100,000 in 50 years to 70,000. The worst thing about the floods is their **unpredictability**, and that they cost the city $5 million annually in lost work hours. **Priceless** frescoes are subject to damp and are at risk of permanent water damage; tourists find they have wet feet in St Mark's Square 50 times a year. This flooding is most **dramatic** when a higher-than-average tide **coincides** with various other **phenomena** – such as heavy rainfall inland from the Venetian lagoon, a wind blowing in from the Adriatic Sea or an area of low pressure.

High water is most likely to occur between September and April, though it's not unheard of at other times. July is just about the only dry month in a city of water built in a lagoon in the Adriatic Sea. If you are a tourist planning ahead, you can expect the highest tides around the time of a full moon or a new moon. When a level above 110 cm is expected – which will invade nearly 12% of Venice – sirens will sound a warning 3–4 hours in advance of high tide, with an increasing number of tones to signify every 10 cm above 110 cm, warning residents to protect their properties and get out their wellington boots. The speakers are concealed inside bell towers and public buildings.

For half a century there has been constant debate on how to save the city, but no agreement can be reached, not even on whether the situation is getting worse. The number of high tides varies between 80 and 100 in **consecutive** years, without any

apparent **trend**; the worst flood of 194 cm was in 1966, but in 2001 there was a high tide of 144 cm. What is certain is that the Adriatic has risen by 23 cm over the last 50 years, after decades of **stability**. This may be due to global factors, or to heavy draining of underground water by local factories; an **aggravating** factor is that the city also suffers from subsidence.

Venice has twin problems of subsidence and rising water levels. The **current** plan to **alleviate** flooding consists of giant gates at the entrances to the lagoon. Many locals believe the development is a waste of money and may even worsen the situation. This remains to be seen, but Venice is certainly one of the world's first major cities to be threatened by rising sea levels due to climate change.

Paintings by Venice's most famous artist, Canaletto, show how much the sea has risen around the city in the years since his death in 1768: 80 cm, an average of 2.4 mm annually. His paintings are so realistic that they include tidemarks on the buildings beside canals, and are as accurate as photographs since he used a *camera obscura* to project images through a lens on to his canvases.

When the tide is high, the boats cannot pass under the bridges, and kilometres of temporary raised wooden walkways (*passerelle*) have to be laid to keep feet dry, though these are in danger of being swept away by the high waters and there are particular fears for schoolchildren. There is a plan to install barriers on the seabed by the year 2010, which could be raised as a temporary dike when high tides are predicted, but it is hugely expensive and some experts have warned that the dike might have to go up as many as 200 times a year, and that the barriers could have **adverse** environmental effects on the lagoon.

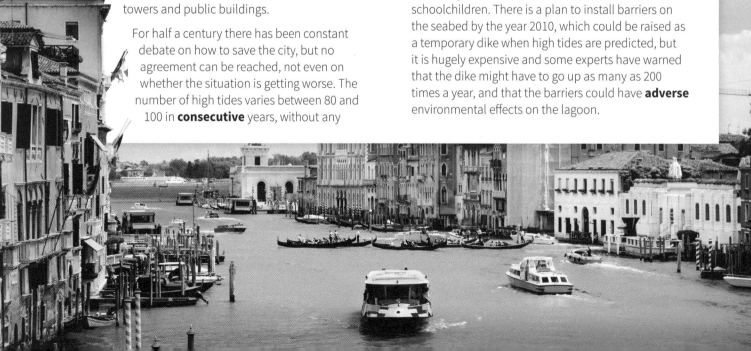

# F Language and style

10  Use the following words, shown in bold in Passage **B**, in sentences of your own which show you understand their meaning. Look up any that you are not sure of.

a  overwhelm _____

_____

b  relentless _____

_____

c  dwindled _____

_____

d  unpredictability _____

_____

e  priceless _____

_____

f  dramatic _____

_____

g  coincides _____

_____

h  phenomena _____

_____

i  consecutive _____

_____

j  trend _____

_____

k  stability _____

_____

l  aggravating _____

_____

m  current _____

_____

n  alleviate _____

_____

o  adverse _____

_____

**11** Add prepositions in the spaces below, then check back in Passage B to see whether your answers are correct.

**a** eating _____ the wooden doors    **e** debate_____how to save

**b** the worst thing _____ the floods    **f** suffers_____ subsidence

**c** subject _____ damp    **g** in danger_____being swept away

**d** at risk _____ permanent water damage    **h** adverse environmental _____the lagoon

**12** Study the use of full stops, semicolons and commas in the first paragraph of Passage B, then fill in the missing punctuation marks in the next two paragraphs, copied below, without looking back until you have finished.

> High water is most likely to occur between September and April though its not unheard of at other times July is just about the only dry month in a city of water built in a lagoon in the Adriatic Sea. If you are a tourist planning ahead you can expect the highest tides around the time of a full moon or a new moon. When a level above 110 cm is expected which will invade nearly 12% of Venice sirens will sound a warning 3 4 hours in advance of high tide with an increasing number of tones to signify every 10 cm above 110 cm warning residents to protect their properties and get out their wellington boots. The speakers are concealed inside bell towers and public buildings.
>
> For half a century there has been constant debate on how to save the city but no agreement can be reached not even on whether the situation is getting worse. The number of high tides varies between 80 and 100 in consecutive years without any apparent trend the worst flood of 194 cm was in 1966 but in 2001 there was a high tide of 144 cm. What is certain is that the Adriatic has risen by 23 cm over the last 50 years after decades of stability. This may be due to global factors or to heavy draining of underground water by local factories an aggravating factor is that the city also suffers from subsidence.

## G Comprehension and summary

**13 a** Which words and phrases does the writer of Passage **B** use to convey the seriousness of the threat to Venice of the high tides?

_____

_____

_____

_____

_____

_____

**b** Which words and phrases does the writer of Passage **B** use to convey the difficulty of finding a solution to the problem?

_____

_____

_____

_____

_____

_____

## H Directed writing

**14** Imagine that you live in Venice. Write a letter to a friend giving an account of the effect of _acqua alta_ on your life and your city.

_____

_____

_____

_____

_____

_____

_____

_____

_____

_____

_____

_____

_____

_____

_____

_____

_____

_____

_____

_____

_____

_____

_____

_____

_____

_____

_____

# 1 Composition

## Descriptive writing

**a** Describe a large public building, such as a castle, palace or hotel, which you have visited and which made an impression on you.

**b** Describe the scene, and your thoughts and feelings, when you arrived in a country you were visiting for the first time.

## Narrative writing

**c** 'I looked back, and saw that the building was now just a heap of rubble.' Write a story with this as the last sentence.

**d** 'The day we moved house'. Write a story with this title.

---

**1** 'Home sweet home'. Discuss the importance of the idea of home, considering a range of connotations and implications of the word.

**2** Write a story that involves a work of art.

_Coursework topics_

# Unit 8: Medical records

## A Reading

**1   Read the article below.**

### Passage A: Dogs to the rescue

If one is asked to think about rescue dogs, those which are likely to come to mind are St Bernards, with brandy kegs around their necks, digging people out of avalanches in the Alps, earthquake dogs sent to Turkey and Greece in recent years, and of course the guide dogs for the blind.

There is a growing body of evidence and opinion that the olfactory capability of canines is as yet underexploited, and that the acute sense of smell of an ordinary hound can be put to better use than finding lost bones: it could be applied to diagnosing cancer and other serious diseases. This first came to the attention of the medical profession in 1989, when the letters page of a medical journal described the case of a woman whose dog's repeated sniffing at a lesion on her leg had led her to seek medical advice; it was diagnosed as a malignant tumour. The dog (a border collie and dobermann cross) had shown no interest in other moles on her owner's body, but spent several minutes a day sniffing the cancerous mole. Eventually the dog tried to bite off the mole, which was the point at which her owner went to the doctor. In the view of the doctors who wrote to the magazine, the possible use of animals with highly developed sensory abilities in cancer diagnosis was worth investigation; surgeon John Church began doing further research and discovered other cases of dogs which had detected malignant growths and saved their owners' lives.

There is another type of patient to whom dogs have proved invaluable: people who have epilepsy. Dogs can reduce the frequency of epileptic seizures by 40% in those who suffer from them, not only because the presence of the friendly animal reduces the stress which brings on the attack, but also because a trained dog has the intuition to sense an imminent attack – by detecting microscopic twitches of the eyes and nervous movements of the hands and arms – and can give warning up to 40 minutes before a seizure or blackout occurs. It fetches the medication and howls until its owner takes it. Diabetics can also be helped by a barked warning and the dog retrieving a bag containing sugar foods. If an attack does occur, the dog presses an alarm button to summon medical aid.

As well as 'seizure alert' dogs, there are a variety of 'disability' dogs who can help their owners dress and can operate control buttons, fetch items, bring the phone and go shopping. They can even load and unload a washing machine. The dogs must be obedient, confident, sociable, well-adjusted and devoted to their owners, who also have to undergo training. It costs roughly $5000 to train a medical support dog, but their ability to perform various household tasks enables their owners to lead a fuller and more independent life.

Research has proved that, in addition to all these canine services to humans, having a dog improves the quality and duration of human lives by reducing stress through the act of stroking and by providing an incentive for daily exercise and fresh air.

## B Language and style

2 Passage A is in a formal style because it is an informative article. Change the phrases below to less formal language.

a *the olfactory capability of canines is as yet underexploited*

_____

b *has the intuition to sense an imminent attack*

_____

c *the quality and duration of human lives*

_____

3 Remind yourself of the use of apostrophes, dashes, brackets, hyphens, colons, semicolons, commas, full stops and capitals in Passage A, then punctuate the passage below.

this is a curious story a doctor in athens who examined a 33 year old woman after she complained of headaches removed a spider which had made its home in her ear doctor evangelos zervas showed video footage he had recorded of the spider inside the womans ear when he examined the patient he was surprised to find a spiders web and then he saw that there was movement the woman drove a motorcycle it appears that this is when it entered her ear because the temperature is ideal there it stayed

## C Comprehension and summary

4 Re-read Passage A. Write a summary of the ways in which dogs can be of service to humans.

_____

_____

_____

_____

_____

_____

_____

_____

_____

_____

_____

## D Directed writing

5 Write an appeal letter for an imaginary charity called Champion Canines. Use information from Passage **A** to explain the work of the organisation and why money is needed.

_____

_____

_____

_____

_____

_____

_____

_____

_____

_____

_____

_____

_____

_____

_____

_____

_____

_____

_____

_____

_____

_____

_____

## E  Reading

**6**  Read the news report below.

### Passage B: Robot doctors perform surgery

Yesterday a team of six French surgeons in New York were able to carry out an intercontinental surgical operation from more than 4000 miles away and across six time zones.

The operation was to remove a gall bladder in Strasbourg, France, using robotics linked to a high-speed telephone line. It was called 'operation Lindbergh', after the American aviator who was the first man to fly solo across the Atlantic.

The operation took 54 minutes and was a complete success, with no risk to the anonymous patient, a 68-year-old French woman. There were 80 people on hand, some at each end in case things went wrong.

The woman's gall bladder was removed by keyhole surgery at the Strasbourg university hospital, using a camera introduced into her body through a small incision. This is now normal practice for keyhole procedures, but the difference was that the surgical team, led by French professor Jacques Marescaux, controlled the movements of the miniature robot from New York.

The time delay between the surgeons' hand movements, transferred to the robot, had to be constant and kept at no more than 200 milliseconds.

#### Robots are the future

It took two and a half years to create the high-power telephone line capable of reducing the delay to an average of 150 milliseconds, almost impossible to detect, by using a fibre-optic line that transmitted 10 megabytes of computer memory per second.

Previous operations were practised on animals before the human surgery was performed.

Medical professors believe that it will soon be possible to perform operations anywhere in the world. The present cost is a million dollars for this kind of robot, but in a few years they will be a normal part of the surgical apparatus in all hospitals.

## F  Language and style

**7**  **a**  Note that *practise* and *practice* both occur in Passage **B**. Study the way the words have been used, then consider the following similar pairs: *advise* and *advice, license* and *licence, prophesy* and *prophecy*. Complete the rule below.

There is a small group of usually two-syllabled words which have a slightly different spelling for

the _____ form and the _____ form. We spell the word with an *s* when

we are referring to the _____, but with a *c* when we are using the _____.

**b** Note the spelling in Passage **B** of *controlled, transferred* and *transmitted*, which double the final consonant before adding *-ed* or *-ing*. List other two-syllable verbs ending in *l, r* or *t*, usually with the stress on the second syllable, which follow the same rule.

_____

_____

_____

_____

_____

_____

**c** Choose the correct spelling in the following pairs by circling the word.

prefered          preferred

offering          offerring

transference     transferrence

reference        referrence

referal          referral

deterent         deterrent

**8** Choose examples from Passage **B** of vocabulary and syntax that convey the idea of risk, and explain why they have this effect.

_____

_____

_____

_____

_____

_____

_____

_____

_____

_____

## G  Comprehension and summary

**9**  Fill in the gaps to complete the summary of Passage **B**. Use your own words.

Surgeons have proved it is possible to _____ operations across thousands of miles

using _____. These are controlled by surgeons transferring movements by means

of high-speed telephone lines via cameras which have been _____ into the patient's

body. Previous _____ have been performed on animals. It took _____

to perfect the technology. Although the cost at present is _____, it is expected that all

hospitals in the future will have such _____.

**10**  Headlines and titles often act as a summary of a text. Think of other short titles that could
have been used for Passages **A** and **B** to summarise their content.

**A** _____

_____

_____

**B** _____

_____

_____

## H  Directed writing

**11**  Write the journal entry of the surgeon Professor Jacques Marescaux after the operation,
commenting on the history, process and success of the procedure.

_____

_____

_____

_____

_____

_____

_____

_____

_____

_____

_____

_____

_____

_____

_____

_____

_____

_____

_____

_____

_____

_____

_____

_____

## ▌ Composition

### Descriptive writing

a Describe waking up in a hospital bed, what you can see and hear around you, and your thoughts and feelings at the time.

b Write a description entitled 'The healer'.

### Narrative writing

c 'As he became conscious, he realised that he was lying on an operating table and faces in white masks were peering down at him ...'. Continue this story.

d Write a story of an emergency medical rescue.

1 Write an argument speech for or against the claim 'Animal experimentation is cruel and can never be justified.'

2 Write a letter to the editor of the newspaper in which Passage **A** was published, engaging with the ideas in the text and giving your view on whether money should be spent on researching the use of dogs in medicine to detect diseases.

*Coursework topics*

# Unit 9: In deep water

## A Reading

**1** Read the article below.

### Passage A: The cave

Caving is a madness. Any sensible person can see this. The idea of squeezing through cracks and fissures, abseiling into deep, dark holes, pulling yourself through 12-cm crawl spaces by your fingers and toes because you can't get enough of an angle to use your knees and elbows is all horrifyingly claustrophobic enough. But getting stuck halfway through, rock above pressing down on your back, rock below pressing up on your chest? It's the geological equivalent of an anaconda's embrace. Panic only makes things worse.

Deep-water diving is equally insane. Humans just aren't designed to survive under the immense weight of water. At any significant depth, the oxygen in air becomes poisonous and the nitrogen becomes narcotic. To adapt, divers must 'water down' the air with helium. They must do this at exactly the right time. Get it wrong and they risk horrible side effects, such as vomiting, amnesia, seizures and worse. The deeper they go, the smaller the margins for error. Any miscalculations, equipment malfunctions or unknowns and they can't simply swim to safety. Gas in the blood stream has to be released slowly to avoid 'the bends'. The bends are bad. And, of course, panic only makes things worse.

Cave-diving combines these two unfathomable pastimes. It offers all the associated horrors of clambering through inhospitable nooks and crannies with all the complexities of being under water. It is routinely described as one of the most dangerous sports on the planet, but unlike all the other contenders for this accolade – proximity flying, base jumping, rodeo-riding and so forth – it is not an adrenaline sport. Cruelly, your safety depends on remaining relaxed. Pulse rates must never quicken. Breathing must never shorten. Zen-like calm is essential, particularly in situations where you don't feel calm at all. What you want is nice and boring. Under water, things happen slowly. If a parachute fails on a base jump, you have seconds to contemplate your fate. If something goes wrong 10 kilometres down an underwater tunnel, you usually have only until your air runs out to find a solution or make your peace.

There were plenty of quite large incidents in the pioneering days of the sport. Before technical advances during the Second World War, you had two options if you wanted to swim through a submerged cave. Option A, you could hold your breath, dive in and hope there was a pocket of air on the other side. Option B, you could invest in the very latest technology – standard diving equipment consisting of a brass helmet and an unwieldy waterproof suit. Option A was risky but Option B had its downsides, too. It required an air supply to be fed through from the surface.

Even with the advent of self-contained breathing apparatus, the sport was hardly unhazardous. Deaths came with faulty equipment, overzealous ambition and, most of all, problems with orientation. Many cave-diving fatalities have occurred when divers kick up silt, lose their way in zero visibility and then run out of air. To reduce the risk, cave-divers follow a guide line (or lay new line if the cave is undiscovered.)

Equipment has improved a lot since the early days, but accidents still happen. Those who do this sport can't stop because they have to know what's around the next corner, even if it is just another tunnel.

From an article by Mat Rudd, *The Sunday Times*, 1st December 2013.

## B Language and style

**2** Write crossword clues for the words below from Passage **A**, which are the answers. You can either give straightforward definitions, bearing in mind the part of speech, or construct cryptic clues using puns or anagrams. You may need to use a dictionary.

**a** claustrophobic_____

_____

**b** narcotic _____

_____

**c** contenders _____

_____

**d** accolade _____

_____

**e** pioneering _____

_____

**3** These are crossword clues. Find the synonymous words in Passage **A** which could be the answers.

**a** failures to work properly _____

**b** cumbersome or awkward to manage _____

**c** arrival _____

**d** excessively keen _____

**e** locational awareness _____

## C Comprehension and summary

**4** **a** Identify the binomial pair (a fixed-order phrase of two synonymous words joined by 'and') and the ironic word usage in paragraph 1.

_____

**b** Identify the binomial pair and the pun in paragraph 3.

_____

**5** **a** Select words and phrases from paragraph 1 which show the writer's attitude to caving.

_____

_____

**b** Select words and phrases from paragraph 2 which show the writer's attitude to cave diving.

_____

_____

c   Summarise in one sentence of your own words what the writer feels about the underwater sports described in Passage **A**.

_____

_____

# D  Comprehension and summary

**6**  Makes two lists of notes, one each for the dangers of diving in Passage **A** and of cave exploration in Passage **B**.

| Dangers of diving | Cave exploration |
| --- | --- |
| _____ | _____ |
| _____ | _____ |
| _____ | _____ |
| _____ | _____ |
| _____ | _____ |
| _____ | _____ |
| _____ | _____ |
| _____ | _____ |
| _____ | _____ |
| _____ | _____ |

# E  Directed writing

**7**  Using the information in Passage **A**, write an encyclopedia entry under the heading of 'Cave-diving'.

_____

_____

_____

_____

_____

_____

_____

_____

_____

_____

8    Read the following extract.

## Passage B: Men overboard!

My first concern was to look for the ship. I glimpsed a black mass disappearing eastward, its lights fading in the distance. I shouted for help, swimming desperately toward the *Abraham Lincoln*. My clothes were weighing me down. I was sinking! Then I found and seized the arm of my loyal friend.

'What about the ship?' I asked.

'As I jumped overboard, I heard the helmsman shout, 'Our propeller and rudder are smashed by the monster's tusk!'

'Then the ship can no longer steer, and we are done for!'

Having concluded that our sole chance for salvation lay in being picked up by the ship's longboats, we had to take steps to wait for them as long as possible. I decided to divide our energies so we wouldn't both be worn out at the same time: while one of us lay on his back, the other would swim and propel his partner forward.

The monster had rammed us at 11 in the evening. I therefore calculated on eight hours of swimming until sunrise. The dense gloom was broken only by the phosphorescent flickers coming from our movements. I stared at the luminous ripples breaking over my hands, shimmering sheets spattered with blotches of bluish grey. It seemed as if we'd plunged into a pool of quicksilver.

An hour later, I was overcome with tremendous exhaustion. My limbs stiffened in the grip of intense cramps and paralysing cold. I tried to call out. My swollen lips wouldn't let a single sound through. I heard my friend cry 'Help!'. Ceasing all movement for an instant, we listened. His shout had received an answer. I could barely hear it. I was at the end of my strength; my fingers gave out; my mouth opened convulsively, filling with brine …

Just then something hard banged against me. I clung to it and was pulled back to the surface. I fainted … then someone was shaking me vigorously.

'Ned!' I exclaimed. 'You were thrown overboard after the collision?'

'Yes, professor, but I was luckier than you and immediately able to set foot on our gigantic whale. I soon realized why my harpoon got blunted and couldn't puncture its hide. This beast is made of plated steel!'

I hoisted myself to the summit of this half-submerged creature that was serving as our refuge. I tested it with my foot. Obviously it was some hard, impenetrable substance; not the soft matter that makes up the bodies of our big marine mammals but a bony carapace, like those that covered some prehistoric animals. The blackish back supporting me was smooth and polished with no overlapping scales. On impact, it gave off a metallic resonance and, incredibly, it seemed to be made of riveted plates. No doubts were possible! This animal, this monster, this natural phenomenon that had puzzled the whole scientific world, that had muddled and misled the minds of sailors, was an even more astonishing one - made by the hand of man! There was no question now. We were stretched out on the back of some kind of underwater boat that took the form of an immense steel fish.

Just then, a bubbling began astern and the boat started to move. We barely had time to hang on to its topside, which emerged about 80 centimetres above water. It was imperative to make contact with whatever beings were confined inside the machine. I searched its surface for an opening, but the lines of rivets were straight and uniform. Moreover, the moon then disappeared and left us in profound darkness. We would have to wait for daylight to find some way of getting inside this underwater boat, and if it made a dive, we were done for!

In the early hours, the vessel picked up speed. We could barely cope with this dizzying rush, and the waves battered us at close range. Our hands came across a ring fastened to its back, and we all held on for dear life. Finally, the long night was over. From inside the boat came noises of iron fastenings pushed aside. One of the steel plates flew up, and a few moments later, eight sturdy fellows appeared silently and dragged us down into their fearsome machine.

This brutally executed capture was carried out with lightning speed. My companions and I had no time to collect ourselves. I don't know how they felt about being shoved inside this aquatic prison, but as for me, I was shivering all over. With whom were we dealing? Surely with some new breed of pirates, exploiting the sea after their own fashion.

From *Twenty Thousand Leagues Under the Sea*, by Jules Verne

## G Language and style

**9 a** Passage **B** contains adjectives used to intensify the drama and danger. List them here.

_____     _____

_____     _____

_____     _____

_____     _____

_____     _____

**b** Comment on the collective effect in the passage of the following verbs:

*seized, smashed, rammed* _____

_____

_____

**c** Comment on the collective effect in the passage of the following nouns:

*monster, beast, creature* _____

_____

_____

**10** Explain how tension has been created in the narrative through setting and event, structure and tone.

_____

_____

_____

_____

_____

_____

_____

_____

_____

_____

11  Punctuate the paragraph of Passsage **B** below, which has had paragraph breaks, inverted commas, commas and semi-colons, apostrophes, question and exclamation marks, and elllipses (triple dots / suspension marks) removed. Use // to show a change of line.

> An hour later I was overcome with tremendous exhaustion. My limbs stiffened in the grip of intense cramps and paralysing cold. I tried to call out. My swollen lips wouldn't let a single sound through. I heard my friend cry Help. Ceasing all movement for an instant we listened. His shout had received an answer. I could barely hear it. I was at the end of my strength my fingers gave out my mouth opened convulsively, filling with brine Just then something hard banged against me. I clung to it and was pulled back to the surface. I fainted then someone was shaking me vigorously. Ned I exclaimed. You were thrown overboard after the collision Yes professor but I was luckier than you and immediately able to set foot on our gigantic whale. I soon realized why my harpoon got blunted and couldn't puncture its hide This beast is made of plated steel

## H Comprehension and summary

12  Describe the character of the professor, drawing inferences from the way he speaks and behaves in the passage. Give evidence to support your description.

_____

_____

_____

_____

_____

_____

_____

13  Highlight in the passage the points to be included, and then write what happened to the professor between late evening and dawn the following morning, in not more than 250 of your own words.

_____

_____

_____

_____

_____

_____

_____

_____

_____

_____

_____

_____

_____

_____

_____

_____

## ❙ Directed writing

**14** Write the professor's journal entry for the events described in the passage, focusing on his changing thoughts and feelings about the 'monster'.

_____

_____

_____

_____

_____

_____

_____

_____

_____

_____

_____

_____

_____

_____

_____

_____

_____

_____

_____

_____

_____

_____

_____

## J Composition

### Descriptive writing

a Describe a dangerous activity that you have participated in or observed.

b 'A narrow escape'. Write a description with this title, focusing on what you could see and hear at the time, and what was going through your mind.

### Narrative writing

c Write a story called 'No fear'.

d Write a story in that someone pushes themselves beyond their limits.

**Coursework topics**

1 Do you think that people should set out to do things which humans were not designed to.

2 Write a story set at sea or in the sea.

# Unit 10: Losing sleep

## A Reading

**1**  **Read the article below.**

### Passage A: Night raider

How can something so small cause so much trouble, making the killer instinct arise in us all? Weighing no more than a speck of dust, it *strikes* before we are even aware of its presence, then wafts off in drunken flight carrying its precious load and singing its high-pitched song of *victory*. Man's public *enemy* number one – the mosquito.

With its long, streaming legs the mosquito floats in the air, **prowling** for a bare arm or leg to bite and feed upon. Even in the darkness, the insect is surrounded by an aura of **evil** as it seeks to take advantage of the sleeping innocent. And yet, its **malice** goes further, for it not only steals a person's blood and leaves an itchy red bump, but sometimes it also injects malaria – a feared and often fatal disease.

Consider the time, trouble and money we spend on fighting this monster. We drape mosquito nets over the bed, we burn mosquito coils, we rub insect repellent into our exposed flesh, we spray aerosol and we swallow anti-malaria pills. We even hunt the creatures all over the room, throwing shoes, pillows and magazines in a barrage of anti-mosquito fire so that we might put an end to the torment brought about by its infuriating buzzing about our ears. Sometimes we get lucky and spot one of the intruders hovering in the turbulence created by our frantic movements and, as it desperately tries to gain a safe altitude, we manage to squash the hated speck in a stinging clap of execution. Our sense of achievement is short-lived though. As we gaze at the bright smear on our hand, we realise that we are looking at our own blood, recently *plundered*.

How do we put an end to this menace? Perhaps we should learn a lesson from this **fiend** and, in addition to putting up screens and defences, we should move into the attack and invade the mosquito's home. If we spray the stagnant pools of water where the mosquitoes breed and make sure than no containers are left around to collect rain water and so provide them with a new home, perhaps we will be able to outwit the mosquito and sleep soundly in our beds at night without fear of an air raid.

## B Language and style

2    **What is the effect of the following in Passage A:**

   **a**   the title *Night Raider*?

   _____

   _____

   _____

   **b**   the words in bold?

   _____

   _____

   _____

   **c**   the words in italics?

   _____

   _____

   _____

   **d**   the rhetorical questions, imperative sentences and non-sentences?

   _____

   _____

   **e**   the use of *we* throughout the passage?

   _____

   _____

3   **a**   Explain the difference between the verbs *raise*, *rise* and *arise*.

   _____

   _____

   _____

   **b**   Give the simple past and past participle form of each of the verbs above.

   _____

   _____

   _____

**c** Use each of the three verbs in a sentence to demonstrate its meaning.

_____

_____

_____

**4** **Fill in the missing prepositions without looking back at Passage A, then check the third paragraph of the passage to see whether you have completed it correctly.**

Consider the time, trouble and money we spend _____ fighting this monster. We drape

mosquito nets _____ the bed, we burn mosquito coils, we rub insect repellent _____

our exposed flesh, we spray aerosol and we swallow anti-malaria pills. We even hunt the creatures

all _____ the room, throwing shoes, pillows and magazines _____ a barrage of

anti-mosquito fire so that we might put an end _____ the torment brought about _____

its infuriating buzzing _____ our ears. Sometimes we get lucky and spot one of the

intruders hovering_____ the turbulence created by our frantic movements and, as it

desperately tries_____ gain a safe altitude, we manage to squash the hated speck

_____ a stinging clap_____ execution. Our sense of achievement is

short-lived though. As we gaze _____ the bright smear_____ our hand,

we realise that we are looking _____ our own blood, recently plundered.

**5** **The last sentence in Passage A is a conditional sentence. Complete the rules describing the functions and use of tenses of the four types of conditional.**

The first conditional uses the _____ tense with the future tense for events which

are _____ . Second conditionals, which use the simple past followed by _____

plus _____ , signify an event which could happen but which is _____ .

Third conditionals, formed with the _____ tense followed by _____

plus _____ , mean that the event is_____ because it

_____ . There are also zero conditionals, using simple present in both clauses, which

refer to _____ .

## C Comprehension and summary

**6** **What other relevant title(s) could you give the passage?**

_____

_____

7    Make a list of ten points from the passage to explain why the writer hates mosquitoes.

i      _____

ii     _____

iii    _____

iv     _____

v      _____

vi     _____

vii    _____

viii   _____

ix     _____

x      _____

## D   Directed writing

8    Write a public health leaflet, consisting of bullet points in full sentences, for the heading
     'Public enemy number one – the mosquito'. Explain in suitable language why and how one
     needs to protect oneself from mosquitoes.

_____

_____

_____

_____

_____

_____

_____

_____

_____

_____

_____

## E Reading

**9** Read the short story extract below.

### Passage B: A terribly strange bed

*The extracts from a gothic horror story describe the beginning of the narrator's sleepless night in a hotel.*

I soon felt not only that I could not go to sleep, but that I could not even close my eyes. I was wide awake, and in a high fever. Every nerve in my body trembled – every one of my senses seemed to be **preternaturally** sharpened. I tossed and rolled, and tried every kind of position, and **perseveringly** sought out the cold corners of the bed, and all to no purpose. Now I thrust my arms over the clothes; now I poked them under the clothes; now I violently shot my legs straight out down to the bottom of the bed; now I **convulsively** coiled them up as near my chin as they would go; now I shook out my crumpled pillow, changed it to the cool side, patted it flat, and lay down quietly on my back; now I fiercely doubled it in two, set it up on end, thrust it against the board of the bed, and tried a sitting posture. Every effort was in vain; I groaned with **vexation** as I felt that I was in for a sleepless night.

What could I do? I had no book to read. And yet, unless I found out some method of **diverting** my mind, I felt certain that I was in the condition to imagine all sorts of horrors; to rack my brain with **forebodings** of every possible and impossible danger; in short, to pass the night in suffering all conceivable varieties of nervous terror.

I raised myself on my elbow, and looked about the room – which was brightened by a lovely moonlight pouring straight through the window – to see if it contained any pictures or ornaments that I could at all clearly distinguish.

[...] There was, first, the bed I was lying in; a four-post bed, with the regular top lined with chintz – the regular fringed valance all round – the regular stifling, **unwholesome** curtains, which I remembered having mechanically drawn back against the posts without particularly noticing the bed when I first got into the room. Then there was the marble-topped wash-stand, from which the water I had spilled, in my hurry to pour it out, was still dripping, slowly and more slowly, on to the brick floor. Then two small chairs, with my coat, waistcoat, and trousers flung on them [...] Then the dressing-table, **adorned** by a very small looking-glass, and a very large pincushion. Then the window – an unusually large window. Then a dark old picture, which the feeble candle dimly showed me. It was a picture of a fellow in a high Spanish hat, crowned with a plume of towering feathers. A sinister **ruffian**, looking upward, shading his eyes with his hand, and looking intently upward [...]

[...] This picture put a kind of constraint upon me to look upward too – at the top of the bed. It was a gloomy and not an interesting object, and I looked back at the picture. I counted the feathers in the man's hat – they stood out in relief – three white, two green. I observed the crown of his hat, which was of conical shape, according to the fashion supposed to have been favoured by Guido Fawkes. I wondered what he was looking up at. It couldn't be at the stars; such a desperado was neither astrologer nor **astronomer**.

From *The Terribly Strange Bed*, by Wilkie Collins.

## F Language and style

**10** Give modern synonyms for the words in bold in Passage **B**.

**a** preternaturally _____

**f** forebodings _____

**b** perserveringly _____

**g** unwholesome _____

**c** convulsively _____

**h** ruffian _____

**d** vexation _____

**i** astronomer _____

**e** diverting _____

**11** List the ways in which suspense and tension have been created in Passage **B**. Consider the effect of the setting, the action and the language.

_____

_____

_____

_____

_____

_____

_____

_____

_____

_____

_____

_____

_____

_____

_____

_____

_____

_____

## G Comprehension and summary

**12** Complete the sentences using ideas from Passage **B**. Remember to put in the necessary commas.

**a** After having _____

_____

**b** Before _____

_____

**c** Not only _____

_____

**d** Even though _____

_____

**e** In spite of _____

_____

## H Composition

### Descriptive writing

**a** Describe a hotel room that has a strange or frightening atmosphere.

**b** Describe the experience of waking up in a different place from where you went to sleep.

### Narrative writing

**c** Write a story set at night in which an enemy attack takes place.

**d** Write a story that begins: 'I knew that I was not going to get any sleep that night'.

**1** Describe in close detail a painting of your own choice.

**2** Write your own gothic horror story called 'A terribly strange bed'.

Coursework topics

# Unit 11: Sub-zero

## A Reading

**1** Read the article below.

### Passage A: Snow comfort

I'm standing on what feels like two fixed skis, holding on to what looks like the back of a wooden chair, yelling with what I hope sounds like authority. I am **bowling along** a snowy path at about 18 kph under the impetus of a team of six husky dogs. Scandinavia offers husky sledging for tourists. **Blessed with** plentiful snow, but **cursed with** a largely flat terrain, the Scandinavian countries market their own winter sports.

The **masterstroke**, however, was the creation of IceHotel. Now a world-famous attraction, it is built **from scratch** every year on the banks of the Torne River, deep in Swedish Lapland and firmly within the Arctic Circle, where the temperature can plunge as low as –50 ºC, and where for days on end in winter the sun does not rise at all. Initially built in 1991 it was the first, and is still the largest, frozen institution. Everything that looks like glass is actually made of ice: the beds, the chandeliers, the glasses for cold drinks. At IceHotel guests stamp about in boots, mittens and snow suits, all provided by the hotel. Your ice bed comes with reindeer skins plus a cosy sleeping bag. Even so, most guests only stay one night before **heading for** warmer accommodation, Santa's secret underground grotto, or the Northern Lights.

In the daytime you can take your pick of the list of Nordic snow sports, chief of which is husky sledging. More than 150 dogs are kept in a giant kennel opposite the hotel. They pull **upward of** 10,000 IceHotel guests during the winter season. The dogs have to be fit but the guests don't; most people are happy not to drive but to just sit in the sledge and be driven. For the more traditional, there is cross-country skiing, and for the more adventurous, lassoing reindeer is one of the options. Going to a wilderness cabin in a snowmobile and staying the night is an opportunity most guests prefer to **pass on**. The **highlight** of this experience is the sauna, so hot that one has to take periodic tumbles in the snow outside.

For a holiday with a difference, it's **hard to beat**, and makes a good topic of conversation when you get back home. Not many people have stayed in a giant luxury igloo or been hurtled across a snowy landscape by a pack of wolf-dogs. I have been invited out much more often since I had these tales to tell!

## B Language and style

**2** **Find synonyms for the following idiomatic words or phrases as used in Passage A.**

**a** bowling along _____

**b** blessed with _____

**c** cursed with _____

**d** masterstroke _____

**e** from scratch _____

**f** heading for _____

**g** upward of _____

**h** pass on _____

**i** highlight _____

**j** hard to beat _____

## C Comprehension and summary

**3** **Write an advertisement for IceHotel in Lapland.**

_____

_____

_____

_____

_____

_____

_____

_____

_____

_____

_____

# D Directed writing

4    Write a letter or email to a friend back home describing your three-day stay in IceHotel.

# E Reading

**5** **Read the journal entries below.**

## Passage B: On thinning ice

Sam Branson, son of the millionaire entrepreneur and owner of the Virgin group, Sir Richard Branson, is on an epic 1200 mile expedition across the Arctic to witness how climate change is affecting one of the world's most remote places. Here are some extracts from his diary of the journey.

### 23rd April

I've just spent my first night sleeping in a tent in the Arctic. I woke up at 7.00 a.m. and the wind was howling. Snow had covered the base of the tent and the sun was up and full. It wasn't too cold inside the tent but once out of your sleeping bag you need to put your clothes on quickly.

I had felt no sense of isolation sleeping out on the ice and only little frissons of fear when there were strange sounds outside – your thoughts turn to polar bears and wolves. I wasn't lonely – I loved it. I felt at peace.

### 24th April

I woke up this morning from a deep sleep. By night-time I feel so exhausted because we're working non-stop but also because the cold takes it out of you. After a long meeting about the expedition, we organised our food rations for the weeks ahead.

Our breakfast consists of granola and oats. Lunch is carbohydrate bars, soup and nuts, and dinner is pasta or rice. Somehow, we have to eat a block of butter a day to keep our energy levels up.

This afternoon Simon and I went to build an igloo. Simon is great. He's one of the three Inuit hunters with our party and he's got a true sense of humour. He knows the environment well and I feel safer having him around. He killed his first polar bear when he was six.

### 28th April

We woke up this morning and left the mountainous valley where we had camped overnight. It was a clear morning with a chill in the air but by 11.00 a.m. the temperature was perfect. We now have a six-day trek across the land in front of us and I think it's going to get much trickier.

### 1st May

The past two weeks have been uncharacteristically warm and sunny for this time of year, but the most dangerous thing is the intensity of the UV radiation, especially coupled with the highly reflective nature of the snow. Exposure of skin and eyes can be a problem so wearing sunglasses is essential.

At around 4.00 p.m. we came to the frozen MacDonald River. The deep, soft snow in the shaded river gorge made travelling arduous but worse was to come. Following the other members of the group, we realised that the ice was very weak. Every now and again we heard loud cracking noises underneath us. It was stomach-churning. The sharp snap sends chills up your body and you hope the crack doesn't catch up with your feet. You want to turn around and look but you can't stop – you have to move forward. If you fall in, you're pretty much finished. The water is so cold – minus 40 °C – that you can freeze in seconds.

(continued)

### 7th May

Last night, I woke to the sounds of the dogs barking. Through the commotion I heard someone shout: 'Polar bear!' A hundred thoughts raced through my mind. How close was it? Was someone hurt? I looked at my watch – it was 2.30 a.m. I jumped out of my sleeping bag. When I emerged I saw the bear was about 15 metres away and surrounded by mist, making it seem somewhat mysterious. The low-lying sun coated its fur in a yellowish light and its breath condensed in the cold air.

The bear stared us down, then started to run towards us. Someone fired a cracker shell into the air. These sound like firework bangers and are very good for scaring away animals. The shells are also powerful enough to kill a person.

The bear was a little startled and stopped its charge but didn't retreat. It looked magnificent – it was the size of a truck but as agile as a cat. We could see it smelling the air and checking us out as it walked closer. When it got to about 7 metres away one of the Inuit guys shot another cracker shell in the air. There are two cracker shells in the gun – the rest is live ammo.

After this second shot was fired the bear was startled but then charged forward again with real purpose. It looked hungry. It was a large male and they don't scare easily. The bear was ready to attack and was showing all the signs of dangerous behaviour. Some more shots were fired. The bear stopped and moved back a little, still eying up his targets.

The Inuit are polar-bear hunters by culture and one of them now ran towards the bear firing live shots just past it. The bear ran away and gradually melted into the snow around him. Wow, what a feeling! Scared, exhilarated, awed. What an impressive creature! It moved with such grace and power. However harmless it seemed, it was a stealth bomber – sleek and beautiful but deadly.

### 8th May

Global warming has consequences for animals at all levels of the Arctic food chain. Population decline anywhere along the chain has a bigger impact in the Arctic than it might in a warmer climate where there are more animals to fill each niche. The increase in non-native species migrating north is also a concern in the warming Arctic. These species compete with native species for limited resources in an already fragile food web, creating more stress on the eco-system as a whole.

### 10th May

Now we have almost reached the end of our journey, I reflected that the battle for the planet as we know it is being played out on the sea ice.

Extra energy being produced around the world is being absorbed into the ocean, increasing sea temperatures and melting the Arctic ice. It means the ice season, which is so important to the Inuit for hunting and travelling, is diminishing – down from eight months to six months. As the Inuit say: 'Yes, shorter winter seasons mean that we'll have to adapt and make do. Our question to you is, "Can your culture adapt when these changes occur?"'

## F Language and style

6   Join sentences together to make one complex sentence for each of the three paragraphs in the diary entry for 24th April in Passage **B**.

i _____

_____

ii _____

_____

iii _____

_____

7   What stylistic features does Sam Branson use to convey a sense of suspense and tension in his account of the meeting with the polar bear in the 7th May extract?

_____

_____

_____

_____

_____

_____

_____

## G Comprehension and summary

8   Write the list of questions an interviewer might ask Sam Branson in order to obtain the information given in the journal extracts.

_____

_____

_____

_____

_____

_____

_____

**9** Rewrite the entry for 8th May in your own words.

_____

_____

_____

_____

_____

_____

_____

_____

**10** In one sentence for each, summarise:

**a** Sam's pleasures in being in the Arctic.

_____

_____

_____

_____

_____

_____

**b** Sam's worries about the future of the Arctic.

_____

_____

_____

_____

_____

_____

## H Directed writing

11  Write a magazine article about Sam Branson's experience, based on the journal entries in
    Passage **B**. Explore his reasons for going on the expedition, what preparations and skills
    were required, what he learned from it and the conclusions he drew from it.

_____

_____

_____

_____

_____

_____

_____

_____

_____

_____

_____

_____

_____

_____

_____

_____

_____

_____

_____

_____

_____

_____

_____

_____

_____

_____

_____

_____

_____

_____

_____

_____

_____

_____

_____

_____

_____

_____

_____

_____

_____

# ▮ Composition

## Descriptive writing

**a** Describe an underwater scene.

**b** Describe the experience of walking through tropical heat in a desert or jungle.

## Narrative writing

**c** Write a story set in the Arctic.

**d** 'They set off late at night through the fast falling snow ...' Continue the story.

**1** A few people, including scientists and politicians, believe that global warming is not caused by human activity and that nothing we do will change the outcome. What are your personal views on global warming?

**2** Write a mystery or horror short story called 'The snowman'.

*Coursework topics*

# Unit 12: The miracle of DNA

## A  Reading

**1  Read the article below.**

### Passage A: The wonders of science

A long gentle 'beep' from a radio collar told the world that yet another species had been *wiped from the face of the planet*. On this occasion in 2000 it was the Pyrenean ibex, or *bucardo*, that had died out: the last one alive had just been crushed beneath a falling tree in a **freak** accident in Spain.

Or was it extinct? Four years earlier, researchers had created Dolly the Sheep by **cloning** DNA and had shown how technology could be extended to many more species. Alberto Fernandez-Arias thought it might be possible to reverse the **looming** extinction of the *bucardos*. He and his colleagues tracked down the last *bucardo* and took cell samples from its ears.

The challenge was to turn these cells into embryos, and within six years his team had created nearly 300 of them. Of these, more than 50 were implanted into **surrogate** mothers, and in 2003 a *bucardo* was born, the first example of a 'de-extinction'. Fernandez-Arias said, 'Soon I hope we will see these beautiful animals once again repopulating the Pyrenees.' A frog that died out 30 years ago in Australia is also being brought back into existence.

The idea that extinct species could be brought back to life – the basis of the plot of Steven Spielberg's film *Jurassic Park* – is no longer the stuff of science fiction. Biologists are planning to resurrect not just recently extinct species but also those that are long dead, including the woolly mammoth, the passenger pigeon, and the great auk, called the 'penguin of the north'.

Is there any point in bringing back a few extinct species when so many living ones – from the Siberian tiger, which is down to the last 500, or Africa's northern white rhino, just five of which are left – are threatened with **imminent** extinction?

Then there is the matter of where to put the revived species. Many animals died out because their habitats were destroyed. Does this mean we will need to rebuild entire landscapes to house them?

And the most important question of all is why we are still allowing so many animals to become extinct in the first place. Should we not be stopping that before bringing species back from the dead?

From an article by Jonathan Leake, *Sunday Times*, 17th March 2013.

## B Language and style

**2**  **a** Why are the words 'beep', 'de-extinction', and 'penguin of the north' in single inverted commas in Passage **A**?

_____

_____

_____

  **b** Why are the words *bucardo* and *Jurassic Park* in italics?

_____

_____

_____

**3**  What is the effect of the use of questions in Passage A?

_____

_____

_____

_____

_____

_____

**4**  Use the following words from Passage **A** in sentences of your own to illustrate their meaning.

  **a** freak (adjective)_____

_____

  **b** cloning (noun)_____

_____

  **c** looming (adjective)_____

_____

  **d** surrogate (adjective)_____

_____

  **e** imminent (adjective)_____

_____

**5** Replace the following phrases from Passage **A** with a single word.

**a** told the world _____

**b** wiped from the face of the planet _____

**c** tracked down _____

**d** basis of the plot _____

**e** the stuff of science fiction _____

## C Comprehension and summary

**6** Write a one-paragraph summary in your own words of what, according to Passage **A**, scientists have already achieved in this field, and what they hope to achieve.

_____

_____

_____

_____

_____

_____

_____

_____

_____

_____

_____

_____

_____

_____

_____

_____

_____

_____

_____

## D Directed writing

7   Write a letter or email to the editor of the newspaper in which Passage **A** was published, giving your views on the practice of bringing extinct animals back to life, using information from the passage.

# E Reading

**8** **Read the fact sheet below.**

## Passage B: DNA

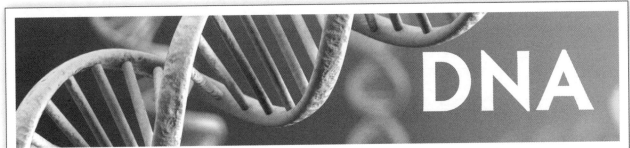

### What is DNA?

- It is a molecule in every cell in our bodies that carries our genetic code and determines our physical and behavioural characteristics.

- It has the shape of a double helix, like a long twisted ladder

- The rungs of the ladder are made of pairs of four molecules called nucleotides.

- Our genetic code is made of 3 billion nucleotides.

- 99.9% of the DNA from two people will be identical. The 0.1% of DNA code sequences that vary from person to person are what make us unique.

- These sequences are called genetic markers, and are the part of the code that forensic scientists use when doing a DNA test. The more closely related two people are, the more likely it is that some of their genetic markers will be similar.

- Identical twins are the only people who have identical genetic markers.

- All cells in the body contain exactly the same DNA, so samples can be taken from almost anywhere in the body, including skin, hair follicles, and blood.

### How does DNA testing work?

- The code is analysed from a clump of molecules in a sample and a DNA 'fingerprint' is created for comparison with another fingerprint.

The chance that two unrelated people could have identical DNA profiles is less than one in a billion.

### What is DNA testing used for?

- Parental testing – to establish if someone is the biological parent of a child.

- Forensic testing – to help identify suspects or victims in a criminal investigation.

- Gene therapy – to test parents or foetuses for genetic conditions or birth defects.

- Genetic genealogy – to find out more about someone's ancestry.

### Examples of how DNA tests have been used

- In the 1950s, a woman claimed to be the Grand Duchess Anastasia, the youngest member and only survivor of the Russian imperial family, executed in 1918. After the woman died, DNA tests proved she was no relation to the Imperial family and her claim had been false.

- DNA evidence convicted the US serial killer Timothy Spencer and also cleared a man wrongly convicted of one of his crimes.

- A four-year-old boy, Bobby Dunbar, who disappeared in 1912, was apparently found a few months later, and was returned to his family, although another woman claimed he was really her son. DNA testing proved in 2004 that he was not Bobby Dunbar.

## F Language and style

**9 a** Rewrite the first section of Passage **B** in four complex sentences, joining related ideas in a single sentence.

_____

_____

_____

_____

_____

_____

_____

_____

**b** Explain the effect of the change of style from simple or compound sentences presented as a list of bullet points to continuous prose consisting of complex sentences.

_____

_____

_____

## G Comprehension and summary

**10 a** Define DNA in one sentence.

_____

_____

_____

_____

**b** Explain in one sentence how it is used.

_____

_____

_____

_____

## H Composition

### Descriptive writing

**a** Describe the moment in a science laboratory when it is discovered that an experiment has gone horribly wrong.

**b** Describe a crime scene.

### Narrative writing

**c** Write a story about how the discovery of DNA changed someone's life.

**d** Write a narrative involving identical twins.

> **1** Research an animal that is under threat of extinction and write an informative and argumentative piece about it, arguing why it should not be allowed to die out.
>
> **2** Write a science-fiction story in which an amazing discovery is made.
>
> *Coursework topics*

# Acknowledgements

The author and publishers are grateful for the permission to reproduce texts in either the original or adapted form. While every effort has been made, it has not always been possible to identify the sources of all the materials used, or to trace all copyright holders. If any omissions are brought to our notice, we will be happy to include the appropriate acknowledgements on reprinting.

p. 72 From *The cave* (Matt Rudd) The Sunday Times, (c) NI Syndication.

p. 97 From *The wonders of science* (Jonathan Leake), The Sunday Times, (c) NI Syndication.

The publishers would like to thank the following for permission to reproduce photographs:

p. 1 DVARG/Shutterstock; p. 4 James Steidl/Thinkstock; p. 8 Hubis/Shutterstock; p. 12 DVARG/Shutterstock; p. 19 rypson/iStock; p. 25 Air Canada; p. 39 WTPix; p. 47 Donovan van Staden/Shutterstock; p. 51 WTPix; p. 47 JRabski/Thinkstock; p. 53 WTPix; p. 55 Marco Simon/Robert Harding; p. 60; Iakov Kalinin/Shutterstock; p. 65 Mike Walker/Rex Features; p.72 Rich Cary/Shutterstock; p. 75 Mustello/Thinkstock; p. 80 (top) Julie de Leseluc/Shutterstock; p. 80 (background) marcovarro/Shutterstock; p. 85 DVARG/Shutterstock; p. 88 Louise Murray/Robert Harding; p. 92 Cubo Images/Robert Harding; p. 101 Dabarti CGI /Shutterstock; p. 103 moodboard/Thinkstock

# Answers

*Note: In some cases more than one correct answer is possible, or students have been asked to write their answers in their own words. Some examples are supplied: they are not prescriptive.*

## Unit 1

**2 & 3 (Sample answers)**

   **a** extravaganza – spectacle (noun)

   **b** coordinated – combined (adjective)

   **c** synchronised – made to happen at the same time (verb)

   **d** technicians – specialists (noun)

   **e** electric – excited (adjective)

   **f** incandescent – fiery (adjective)

   **g** iridescent – sparkling (adjective)

   **h** scintillating – shimmering (adjective)

   **i** mesmerised – entranced (adjective)

   **j** simultaneously – at the same time (adverb)

**4 (Sample answers)**

   **a** Use of same structure in a set of simple sentences gives the effect of a series of separate events, quickly succeeding each other, which replicates the watcher's experience.

   **b** The vocabulary is figurative, creating a series of metaphors describing the role of the tower and the speed of movement of the exploding fireworks. Many of the images are from nature, and these conjure the ideas of colour and beauty.

**5 (Answers may include)**

  Para. 1: time, place and nature of the event

  Para. 2: records broken

  Para. 3: features of the display: countdown; flag; use of the Burj Khalifa

  Para. 4: planning and statistics for the display

  Para. 5: reaction and behaviour of the crowd

  Para. 6: made-up quotation from an organiser and/or spectator

  **7 a** *are believed; have been invented; were used; is believed; thrown; heated; are still made; were enjoyed; were achieved; is less frequently used; were added; was masterminded; set off; was produced and launched; held; are set off; was seen*

   **b (Sample answer)**

   Passives are predominantly used in non-fiction, informative, discursive and scientific writing or speaking, e.g. text books, political texts, instruction manuals. They tend to make expression more tactful, impersonal, formal or objective, and give authority to the text. The emphasis in the sentence falls on the object or event and not on the human agent, who is often unspecified.

8   There are **few** signs of fireworks losing popularity as a form of entertainment. Gradually, private firework shows are becoming **less** common and are being replaced by public events. This means that the injuries caused by fireworks are **fewer**, but they are still a cause of damage to property, unintended fires, maiming of children and traumatising of animals. **A few** people argue that fireworks are destructive in many senses, and that the expense and waste of natural resources cannot be justified in return for **a few** moments of pleasure, but there is **little** public debate on the subject, and unlikely to be, given that they have been around for so long.

*Little* (and its comparative *less* and its superlative *least*) is used before singular or non-countable nouns, like time, whereas *few* (and its comparative *fewer* and its superlative *fewest*) is used before plural and countable nouns, like hours. The indefinite article in the phrases *a little* and *a few* make the effect positive rather than negative. For example, *A few people attended* is more positive than *Few people attended*.

10  **a**  the 13th

**b**  **(Sample answer)**

The addition of metals to gunpowder gave fireworks a wider range of colours and made them burn with sparks.

**c**  Kuwait

**d**  **(Sample answer)**

The speed of sound is much slower than the speed of light.

**e**  **(Sample answers)**

i   summon/conjure up wealth

ii   different coloured fireworks were a novelty/new invention

iii   continue to lead the way/initiate developments

11  **(Sample answers)**

**a**  The Chinese probably invented fireworks two millennia ago – perhaps accidentally and are now the main producer of fireworks (despite the dangers involved in their manufacture by hand), which are used in their many festivals, including celebrations of New Year and to commemorate the invention of the firecracker.

**b**  Italy took a particular interest in fireworks, developing them in the 19th century. It is still being at the cutting edge of pyrotechnics and involved in major displays today.

**c**  Fireworks consist of gunpowder (saltpetre, charcoal and sulphur) mixed with various chemical compounds, depending on the colours and sounds desired, within a cardboard shell.

12  **(Sample answer)**

Originating in the Far East in ancient times, the knowledge of gunpowder moved westwards and became known in Europe in the medieval period, when more colours were made possible by the addition of other chemicals. By the 19th century, a range of types of firework had been developed, including those with sound effects. Displays continually increase in length and spectacle, thanks to the recent use of computers to coordinate them and to add music, and fireworks are now used worldwide to celebrate local, national and international events.

**13** **(Answers may include)**

fireworks cause injury (blindness and maiming); waste of natural resources, such as magnesium; only last a few minutes but cost a phenomenal amount; money could be spent on something lasting and worthwhile; primitive behaviour to get excited about fire; trauma caused to wildlife and domestic animals; encourages bad feeling and one-upmanship between countries.

# Unit 2

**3** (Note that alternatives are possible. The important thing is to mark the beginning and end of the parenthesis in the right place.)

**a** Wild apes have no need of language, and have not developed it, but tame ones can use it as a tool for communicating with each other.

**b** Each slaughtered ape is a loss to the local community – a loss to humanity as a whole – and is a hole torn in the ecology of our planet.

**c** The skills of language and counting – essential for negotiating trade – can be taught to orang-utans, who are less social primates than chimpanzees, in a matter of weeks.

**d** Fifteen million years (a small gap in the broad scale of evolution) is an immense period in terms of everyday life.

**e** Gorilla mothers prefer to cradle their babies on their left sides – a feature shared with humans – and there have been cases of them showing maternal behaviour to human children.

**4** **a** T          **b** D          **c** D          **d** T          **e** F

**5** **b** (Sample answer)

Teddies were named after US President Theodore Roosevelt, who refused to shoot a cornered bear when out hunting in Mississippi in 1902. After a newspaper cartoonist had made the hunting story famous, a New York shop owner was granted permission by the President to name the bears in his shop, made by his wife, 'Teddy's Bears'.

**8** (Sample answers)

**a** We are told that the bear was not usually chained during the day and can infer that he did not like being chained, so we would expect him to break free. By calling it *the bear* in paragraph 5, the writer implies that it is the same one. We do not expect a wild bear to accept being hit with an umbrella. We are told that on her return the lady's bear was *looking very sorry for himself*, which suggests that he was the bear who had been hit.

**b** He had been found *small and helpless* and *half-dead of hunger*. Although the bear was strong, he was gentle and friendly, and loved by dogs, children and the cook. He disliked being on a chain but was *good as gold* about it. The lady had punished him previously by making his nose bleed. It was unfair of her to threaten to deprive him of his favourite food of apples because of her own mistake.

**9** (Sample answers)

**a** A woman owned a full-grown pet bear, which she chained up when she went out. One Sunday she met a bear in the forest on her way to her sister's house and, assuming it was her bear, she scolded and hit it for having broken its chain and followed her. The bear went away, but when the lady arrived home and found her bear still chained up, she was told by her cook that he had never left, and she then realised that she had attacked a different bear.

**b** Cubs are considered appealing and vulnerable. They appear in popular children's fiction, and their image is widely used commercially. They can be tamed and kept as pets. Like children, they like sweet foods. They seem to have friendly eyes, and look cuddly. They are playful and tolerant, and get on with other animals and children.

# Unit 3

**2**   **a** respective   **b** mainly   **c** part   **d** vital   **e** sort out

**4**   **(Sample answers)**
   **a** situation  **b** supervise  **c** correct  **d** equivalents  **e** response  **f** thoroughly

**5**   **a**   sub, ad, con, re, per, extro, co, o, a
   **b**   re, im, de, ex, pur, sup, trans
   **c**   re, in, con
   **d**   re, ab, con, dis, pre
   **e**   im, com, re, sup, ap

**6**   **Sentences should contain the following words with their correct meanings.**
   **a**   proceed (go forward); precede (go before)
   **b**   lie (no object); lay (with object)
   **c**   affect (verb); effect (noun)
   **d**   continuous (without breaks); continual (with breaks)
   **e**   principal (adjective meaning main); principle (noun meaning fundamental belief)
   **f**   whose (belonging to whom); who's (contraction of who is or who has)
   **g**   uninterested (not interested); disinterested (not biased)

**7**   **a**   Dashes have a space either side and are used singly to *add on an apparently spontaneous afterthought*. For example: *There were hundreds of people there – maybe thousands.*
   **b**   Hyphens, which do not have spaces before or after, are used to *join two or more words together in a compound, to show that their meaning is dependent on each other.* For example: *mother-in-law, old-fashioned.*

**8**   **a**   The article is aimed at readers of a careers or in-flight magazine who may have an interest in the job.
   **b**   **(Sample answer)**
   The informal style includes: compound sentence structures; sentences beginning with *So* and *And*; the use of ellipsis for dramatic effect; missing verb *to be* (*three aircraft in Leeds and their corresponding passengers in Manchester*); questions and exclamations; single dashes; non-technical/non-specialist vocabulary; contracted verb forms (*it's, what's*);

**9**   **(Sample answer)**
   TopFlights charters operate out of two airports in the UK, but principally Manchester, where it is well established and the third-largest airline. It runs scheduled, high-frequency, short-distance flights. Punctuality is a high priority for the company.

**10**   **(Sample answer)**
   Airport managers should be calm and organised, versatile and flexible. They must be efficient across a range of skills, contexts and interactions with people. Good communication skills and a sense of humour are necessary qualities.

**11 (Sample answer)**

The job of an airport manager is to adhere to the standards of the company, to monitor processes to ensure efficient functioning, and to activate the correction of weaknesses through staff training. They must keep informed, pass on information to the company and collaborate with other airport managers for their airline. They must consider the image of the company they represent.

**14 (Sample answers)**

**a** So that if they get separated from their 'auntie' they can explain who they are and their parents can be contacted.

**b** In case your child needs to buy something in the airport or on the plane.

**c** To familiarise your child with the place so that s/he feels less apprehensive about the experience next day.

**d** To avoid large crowds which might be overwhelming for your child.

**e** Because children are likely to feel more homesick and frightened at night.

**f** In case the flight is delayed or cancelled and your child needs to be returned to you.

**g** So that your child does not feel trapped amongst strangers and can go to the toilet easily.

**h** Your child will feel less daunted if they can see and hear other children.

**17 (Answers may include)**

Para. 1: Explain why you are writing and where you saw the advertisement.

Para. 2: Give your qualifications.

Para. 3: Explain how your skills fit the job description and why you would make a suitable employee.

Para. 4: Thank the recipient for their attention and say that you hope to be called for an interview.

# Unit 4

**2** (Sample answers)

**a** We use apostrophes either when we wish to signify omission of letters (for example *can't, six o'clock*) or when we wish to show possession (for example: *one week's time, the dog's tail*). An apostrophe after the final *s* of a word, unless it is a name, indicates that the possessor is plural (for example: *the girls' books*).

**b** We use an apostrophe in *it's* if the meaning is *it is* or *it has*, whereas *its* without an apostrophe is used to show possession (for example: *the dog wagged its tail*) (compare to *his* and *hers*).

**3** (Sample answer)

Semicolons, which are used sparingly and only for a good reason, have the same function as full stops but are used when the preceding sentence has a close connection with the following sentence. They can also be used to separate items in a list.

**5** (Sample answer)

Ancient civilisations played a kind of football and exported the game to their empires. Football as we know it dates from late 12th-century England. In 1863, after a brief lapse, it was re-established when the Football Association was set up. By the 1870s, professional teams existed, which played internationally in South America and northern Europe. FIFA evolved as an organisation, resulting in the World Cup. The modern game owes much to mass-media coverage – which began in 1927 – and consequent financial influence.

**6** (Answers should include a consideration of the alternative arguments.)

**8** **a** niche – specialised

**b** corruption – debasement

**c** asymmetrical – lopsided

**d** proficient – accomplished

**e** tactical – strategic

**9** Within speech, most of the same punctuation rules apply as for normal writing, so that there needs to be a **full stop** at the end of a sentence, provided that there is no continuation of the sentence after the end of the speech. If there is, then in place of the full stop we use a **comma** or, if appropriate, a question mark or exclamation mark. Even after a question or exclamation mark, the next word begins with a **lower-case** letter rather than a **capital** if it is continuing the sentence. If a sentence in speech is interrupted and then continued, there is a **comma** before the break and again before the re-opening of the inverted commas. The continuation will begin with a small letter, not a capital because the **sentence** is also continuing. There must always be a punctuation mark of some kind before the closing **inverted commas**. If a speech contains speech or quotation, then the inner speech must use the opposite kind of **inverted commas** from the outer speech, whether single or double.

**10** After a single vowel, the consonant will double if the vowel sound is short (for example: *dinner* with a short vowel sound; *diner* with a long vowel sound).

**11** *fore-* front, before

*medi-* middle

*sym-* alike

*para-* equal

*en-* into

**12** **a** on the up – becoming more popular

**b** not inconsiderable – significant

**c** a cross between – a mixture of

**d** from time to time – occasionally, periodically

**e** give it a go – have a try at it

**14** **Points to include:**

**a** Historical background: name means 'royal'; first type of tennis and other ball games played on a court; the game of kings; played on huge indoor courts; started in medieval France; taken to England in early 16th century; now has 10,000 players; played in four countries; little played for most of 20th century; has grown in popularity recently.

**b** Unusual features: asymmetrical court with buttress; courts differ in size; mixture of modern tennis and squash; unusual rules; suits less fit players; balls are heavy; ball comes from different directions; game of strategy more than physical skill.

# Unit 5

**2**

| Noun | Adjective | Verb | Adverb |
|---|---|---|---|
| produce, producer, product, production | productive | **produces** | productively |
| **occurrence**, recurrence | current | occur, recur | recurringly, currently |
| depth | **deep** | deepen | deeply |
| **origins** | original | originate | originally |
| **explorers**, exploration | exploratory, explorative | explore | exploratively |
| measure, measurement | measurable, measured | **measured** | measurably |
| sponsor, sponsorship | sponsored | **sponsored** | |
| conviction, convict | convicted, convincing | **convinced**, convict | convincingly |
| definition | definite, finite | define | **definitely** |
| extreme, extremity, extremist | **extreme** | | extremely |

Note: when a two-syllabled noun and a verb are spelt the same, the noun is often stressed on the first syllable and the verb on the second, e.g. _pro_duce and pro_duce_, _con_vict and con_vict_.

**3**  **a**  to separate clauses (e.g. _The precise source of the Amazon was only recently discovered, although the origins of most of the earth's great rivers have been known for some time ..._ )

   **b**  to create a clause in apposition, (e.g. _the mouth of the Amazon, where it meets the sea, is so deep as well as wide ..._ )

   **c**  to create a parenthesis (e.g. _A global positioning system (GPS), linked to a network of satellites, was employed ..._ )

   **d**  to separate items in a list (e.g. _because of a combination of unfriendly terrain, high altitudes, cold winds ..._ )

   **e**  after an initial adverb (e.g. _Famously, the Amazon river is home to many exotic ..._ )

**4**  **b**  (Sample answers)

   The source of the Amazon, which has only recently been discovered, although explorers tried for centuries to discover it, is located 160 km from the Pacific Ocean.

   Although explorers tried for centuries to discover the source of the Amazon, it has only recently been discovered, located 160 km from the Pacific Ocean.

   Located 160 km from the Pacific Ocean, the source of the Amazon, only recently discovered, was sought by explorers for centuries.

   Having searched for it for centuries, explorers recently discovered the location of the source of the Amazon, 160 km from the Pacific Ocean.

5   **(Sample answer)**

The tropical Amazon is fed by torrential rains and thereby produces a fifth of the world's river water – much more than that of the longest river, the Nile. The Amazon is not only the world's widest river, owing to seasonal floods, with an average width of 8 km and a depth which makes it navigable far inland, but it is also the second longest, at roughly 6300 km.

8   **a**   *impenetrable, inscrutable intention, gloom of overshadowed distances, you lost your way, bewitched, cut off for ever*

   **b**   *mob, unrestful and noisy, overwhelming realities, implacable force, brooding, vengeful aspect*

9   **(Sample answer)**

Passages A and B are informative. The extract about the River Congo is literary and lyrical, i.e. its aim is to create atmosphere and evoke feelings, to convey facts. It achieves this by using figurative language: similes; metaphors; multiple adjectives; emotive vocabulary; alliteration; anthropomorphism (ascribing human characteristics to objects); use of the second person; reflections; repetition for effect. These are some of the characteristics of descriptive writing.

10   **Facts**

- essential to support life
- covers 4% of country
- most Egyptians live on its banks
- provides water for crops and cattle
- floods every July
- 7000 km long
- river mouth in Cairo
- contains crocodiles
- source discovered mid-19th century
- transport for building of pyramids
- mentioned in the Bible
- used for book and film settings
- attracts tourists
- polluted by chemicals
- continuous building along banks

**Fictions**

- belongs to the god Isis
- pharaohs controlled it with magical powers
- inhabited by half-human, half-fish creatures
- owned by creatures who must be kept happy
- snakes created from its mud
- leisure boats have polluted it

**11 Similarities**

- very long
- floods seasonally
- contains vicious animals
- flows through jungle
- has elusive source

**Differences**

- Amazon carries more water
- Nile does not receive much rainfall
- different altitude
- different climate zone
- inhabitants depend on Nile
- Nile has been literary inspiration
- Nile attracts mass tourism
- Nile is polluted
- source of Amazon discovered only recently

# Unit 6

2 **(Sample answers)**

    **a** raising

    **b** labours

    **c** provisions, board

    **d** skill , proficiency

    **e** valid

    **f** sanction, condone

    **g** struggle

    **h** confined

3   **a** together, for example *connect, conflict*

    **b** before, for example *preparation, predestined*

    **c** forward, for example *propel, propose*

    **d** across, for example *transmit, transitory*

    **e** inside, for example *intravenous, introspective* (Note: *intransigent* has *in* as a negative prefix before another prefix, *trans*, and not a prefix *intra*).

    **f** outside, for example *extravagant, extraordinary*

    **g** out, for example *exhale, extinguish*

    **h** again, for example *review, restore*

    **i** between, for example *intersperse, intercept*

    **j** to put into, for example *endanger, encircle*

4   **a** three           **i** 12

    **b** two              **j** 20

    **c** ten              **k** 14

    **d** eight           **l** three

    **e** five            **m** seven

    **f** two             **n** one

    **g** one            **o** 144.

    **h** four

**5** **(Answers may include)**

- elephant called Noppakhao/Peter is an artist in Thailand who has painted a self-portrait
- has painted dozens of works over last few years of fellow elephants and natural subjects
- considered similar to Picasso in his style and use of colour
- prefers representative pictures to abstract ones
- some paintings have been sold for $700
- description of site/project/*mahout*
- description of method/tools of his painting
- meaning of his name
- character description
- quote by AEACP

**9**  **a** **(Sample answers)**

The moral of the story is that when one only has part of the picture one cannot see the whole truth.

Those who fight in the belief they are right should get together with others who have different but equally valid beliefs.

The truth is always bigger than we can see with at first.

Human beings working alone do not arrive at the total solution.

We are all as limited in our perception of the whole truth as a blind person.

**9**  **b** **(Sample answer)**

Six blind men, who were friends but competitive and who each thought they knew best, went on a trip to a zoo, where they unknowingly encountered an elephant. The six men each formed a judgement, after handling only one part of it, in turn, that it was a different object: a wall, a snake, a rope, a tree, a sword, a fan. They were arguing so much that the zookeeper heard them and arrived to recapture the elephant. The zookeeper solved the mystery by telling them that it was an elephant, and that each of them was partly right but also entirely wrong. [103 words]

# Unit 7

**2** **(Sample answers)**

| | | |
|---|---|---|
| **a** surveyed | **e** exposed | **i** deconstruct, take to pieces |
| **b** in complete agreement | **f** integral, essential | **j** reducing, decreasing |
| **c** deep | **g** future generations | |
| **d** hazardous, dangerous | **h** irreversibly | |

**3** **a** reunited   **b** removed   **c** reciprocal   **d** resist   **e** restitution
   **f** rewound   **g** relocation   **h** repatriation   **i** retrograde   **j** resources

**4** For a completed and dated action in the past we use the <u>past simple</u>, whereas for an action which began in the past but which is not yet completed we use the <u>present perfect</u>. The past perfect tense is used when an action <u>occurred before another action in the past</u>. The past continuous shows that an action <u>was already occurring</u> when <u>another action interrupted it</u>.

**5** **a** I visited the exhibition, which I heard about on the radio.
   **b** I read about the man who had stolen the statues.
   **c** I bought a book which was about the history of Greece.
   **d** I met Lord Byron, who had written a poem the previous day.
   **e** We have not visited Greece, which we have heard is a beautiful country.
   **f** I spoke to a woman in the gallery who(m) I had met previously.
   **g** It is difficult to find the people who are responsible for the damage.
   **h** This is the Museum Director, who is against the return of the marbles.
   **i** They didn't find the sculpture(,) which was buried by an earthquake.
   **j** You should have interviewed Lord Elgin, who(m) I introduced to you.

**6** **a** 100%.
   **b** They were loaded on board ships to take them to Britain, and one of the ships sank.
   **c** The Tasmanians.
   **d** Removal, pollution, cleaning.
   **e** Disapproval of their having been stolen; celebration of them as works of art.

**7** **(Answers may include)**
   • an argument supporting the Greek claim to the marbles
   • the British Museum's rationale for retaining them
   • explanation of what the marbles consist of why they are important
   • history of the marbles
   • description of attempts to remove them
   • case for their return to Greece
   • previous reasons for not returning them
   • implications for future of museum property

**11** **a** into   **b** about   **c** to   **d** of   **e** on (about)   **f** from   **g** of   **h** on

**12** High water is most likely to occur between September and April, though it's not unheard of at other times. July is just about the only dry month in a city of water

built in a lagoon in the Adriatic Sea. If you are a tourist planning ahead, you can expect the highest tides around the time of a full moon, or a new moon. When a level above 110 cm is expected – which will invade nearly 12 per cent of Venice – sirens will sound a warning three–four hours in advance of high tide, with an increasing number of tones to signify every 10 cm above 110 cm, warning residents to protect their properties and get out their wellington boots. The speakers are concealed inside bell towers and public buildings.

For half a century there has been constant debate on how to save the city, but no agreement can be reached, not even on whether the situation is getting worse. The number of high tides varies between 80 and 100 in consecutive years, without any apparent trend; the worst flood of 194 cm was in 1966, but in 2001 there was a high tide of 144 cm. What is certain is that the Adriatic has risen by 23 cm over the last 50 years, after decades of stability. This may be due to global factors, or to heavy draining of underground water by local factories; an aggravating factor is that the city also suffers from subsidence.

**13 a** Vocabulary and imagery suggest attack – *fears, threatens, danger, overwhelm, relentless, eating into*

Emotive language evokes pity – *drowning home, schoolchildren*.

*Priceless* conveys the irreplaceable loss of the art treasures.

The use of statistics shows how real the threat is – *the population has dwindled by 100,000 in 50 years to 70,000; 80 cm; 5 million dollars; 50 times a year*.

**b** *Unpredictability* means that Venetians cannot be properly prepared for the high tides.

Uncertainty and disagreement make finding a solution difficult – *constant debate, no agreement, without any apparent trend, half a century*.

The *aggravating factor* of subsidence makes matters seem worse.

The *hugely expensive* cost is an obstacle to finding an acceptable solution – *200 times a year*.

The consequences could be adverse – *experts have warned, environmental effects upon the lagoon*.

**14 (Sample answer)**

Every winter we are afraid that our city will be drowned by the high tides. These are destroying the buildings and forcing Venetians to leave the city, or to move from the ground floor to a higher one. It is frightening not to know when the next high water will come, and we fear for our children's safety. Not only historic buildings but also art treasures are being damaged, which will affect tourism. The city is losing a lot of money because of citizens not being able to get to work when the water level is too high. The sea continues to rise, but no one really knows how we can save our city.

119

# Unit 8

**2** **(Sample answers)**

   **a** so far, insufficient use has been made of the smelling power of dogs

   **b** can predict that a fit is about to happen

   **c** the standard and length of our lives

**3** (Note that variations are possible with the punctuating of parentheses and full-stop versus semi-colon usage.)

This is a curious story: a doctor in Athens who examined a 33-year-old woman, after she complained of headaches, removed a spider which had made its home in her ear. Doctor Evangelos Zervas showed the video footage he had recorded of the spider inside the woman's ear. When he examined the patient, he was surprised to find a spider's web – and then he saw that there was movement. The woman drove a motorcycle; it appears that this is when it entered her ear. (Because the temperature is ideal, there it stayed.)

**4** **(Sample answer)**

Trained dogs can rescue victims of avalanches and earthquakes, as well as guide the blind. Recently it has been discovered that they can detect serious disease by smell. They can also predict and give warning of epileptic seizures and diabetic comas, fetch medication and summon aid. Their ability to perform a variety of household tasks enables the disabled to lead a fuller life. By reducing stress and encouraging exercise, dogs can extend the lives of all dog-owners.

**7** **a** There is a small group of usually two-syllable words which have a slightly different spelling for the <u>verb</u> form and the <u>noun</u> form. We spell the word with an *s* when we are referring to the <u>verb</u>, but with a *c* when we are using the <u>noun</u>.

      Note that American English use of 's' and 'c' in these words is different.

   **b** enrol, patrol, extol; refer, prefer; emit, omit, permit, submit, admit

      Note also travel – travelling; jewel – jewellery; pedal – pedalling

      Note that American English does not double the consonant in the last three and other similar cases.

   **c** preferred, offering, transference, reference, referral, deterrent

**8** • *4000 miles* and *six time zones* create idea of distance

   • reference to Lindbergh emphasises uniqueness of event

   • *80 people on hand* makes clear that an emergency was prepared for

   • *had to be kept constant* and the precision of *200 milliseconds* stress the small margin for error allowed

   • technological data in paragraph 6 emphasises scientific expertise required

   • reference to animal experiments suggests that it was considered a risk for humans

**9** **(Sample answer)**

Surgeons have proved it is possible to <u>conduct/perform</u> operations across thousands of miles using <u>remote-control devices</u>. These are controlled by surgeons transferring movements by means of high-speed telephone lines via cameras which have been inserted into the patient's body. Previous <u>trials/experiments</u> have been performed on animals. It has taken a quarter of a <u>decade</u> to perfect the technology. Although the cost at present is <u>excessive/prohibitive</u>, it is expected that all hospitals in the future will have such <u>equipment/facilities</u>.

**11** **(Sample answer)**

I am very pleased and relieved that today's operation on a woman in Strasbourg was successful and without incident. The medical team was not sure that such a procedure would be possible, although keyhole surgery is now well established, because it has never been achieved on humans before at such a distance. The difficulty was in keeping the time delay constant and very short, and it has taken several years to create a powerful enough fibre-optic telephone line. Many staff were available at both ends in case there was a problem, but it all went according to plan. I think this was the first of many such operations.

# Unit 9

2 **(Sample answer)**

claustrophobic: (simple) *afraid of confined spaces*; (cryptic) *I curb class photo*

3 **a** malfunctions   **b** unwieldy   **c** advent   **d** overzealous   **e** orientation

4 **a** unfathomable; nooks and crannies

   **b** cracks and fissures; embrace

5 **a** *insane*; *horrible side effects*; *the bends are bad*

   **b** *madness*; *horrifyingly claustrophobic*; *an anaconda's embrace*

   **c** The writer does not understand why anyone would want to take part in these highly unpleasant and dangerous activities.

6 Dangers of diving - poisonous oxygen, falling asleep, wrong air mix, nausea, amnesia, fits, the bends, panting, faulty equipment, running out of air.

   Dangers of cave exploration - narrow cracks, dark holes, tight tunnels, claustrophobia, panic, unrealistic aims, losing sense of direction, poor visibility.

7 **(Sample answer)**

Cave-diving

This activity combines the exploration of caves and potholes with underwater diving. Both are considered to be dangerous sports, and the combination makes cave-diving much more so because of the possibility of becoming trapped, running out of air or suffering the side effects of poisonous air, and the necessity for precise timing. The main hazard is loss of orientation, causing the explorer to travel in the wrong direction. Divers must resurface slowly from a great depth in order to avoid damage to the body. Unlike in other extreme sports, a rush of adrenalin is not advantageous or enjoyable, as it is a requirement for safety to stay relaxed and not to panic. When the sport first began, without the benefit of technical aids and using heavy and awkward diving suits, there were many accidents. The use of a guideline is still considered to be a sensible precaution.

9 **a** *sole*; *dense*; *tremendous*; *intense*; *paralysing*; *single*; *gigantic*; *astonishing*; *immense*; *profound*; *dizzying*; *fearsome*

   **b** *seized, smashed, rammed* These verbs convey the violence of the attack on the ship and the desperation of those who fell overboard.

   **c** *monster, beast, creature* These nouns imply that they were attacked by a huge, hostile and horrific animal.

**10** **(Examples of suitable points)**

fading lights, set in late evening, nearly drowns twice, attack by a vicious 'monster'; ship unable to return, long wait, darkness descends, exhaustion and loss of voice (to show helplessness), use of ellipses (to show loss of control), an unknown 'something' and 'it' (only later turns into 'someone' and reader assumes it is the monster); cry for help; frequent use of exlamations (to show fear and amazement); discovery that 'gigantic whale' is made of impermeable steel (making it both unnatural and indestructible); use of triplet (*This animal, this monster, this natural phenomenon*); sudden spurt of speed and fear of falling off; uniformity of the 'beast' (suggesting military capability); disappearance of the moon; reference to 'whatever beings' (suggesting non-humans); unnatural silence of the eight men; suddenness and efficiency of the 'capture', being imprisoned; the unknown fate awaiting the three (outnumbered) captives; the fearful question 'With whom were we dealing?'

**11** An hour later, I was overcome with tremendous exhaustion. My limbs stiffened in the grip of intense cramps and paralysing cold. I tried to call out. My swollen lips wouldn't let a single sound through. I heard my friend cry 'Help!'. Ceasing all movement for an instant, we listened. His shout had received an answer. I could barely hear it. I was at the end of my strength; my fingers gave out; my mouth opened convulsively, filling with brine …

Just then something hard banged against me. I clung to it and was pulled back to the surface. I fainted … then someone was shaking me vigorously.

'Ned!' I exclaimed. 'You were thrown overboard after the collision?'

'Yes, professor, but I was luckier than you and immediately able to set foot on our gigantic whale. I soon realized why my harpoon got blunted and couldn't puncture its hide. This beast is made of plated steel!'

**12** The professor seems an exuberant character, judging from his use of exclamations. He is sensible enough to realise they might need to wait a long time, and that they should conserve their energy; he decides how best to do it, and makes the necessary calculation, evidence that he is educated and used to being in charge. He is able to appreciate the beauty of the sea at night, even in his desperate situation. His physical state seems less robust than that of the other swimmers, as he loses his strength and succumbs to exhaustion. His analysis of the 'carapace' of the 'creature' is scientific and uses technical language; his deductions lead him to arrive at a conclusive judgement that they were dealing with an 'immense steel fish'. He is used to being precise in his observations, giving 80 cms as the distance the 'fish' was protruding from the surface.

**13** Points to be included:

fell overboard as a result of the impact of a supposed whale attack on the Abraham Lincoln at 11pm; found his friend in the water; shared swimming with him for an hour; became too weak and too cold to continue; lost his voice; mouth filled with seawater; started to lose consciousness and drown; returned to surface by holding on to something; was brought round by a sailor called Ned who explained that it wasn't really a whale; climbed on top and investigated what it was made of; had to hold on tight when the submarine picked up speed; buffeted by waves; at dawn, eight men came out of the machine and quickly took professor and companions down into it.

# Unit 10

**2** **(Sample answers)**

    **a** The effect of the title is to make the reader expect it to be about a dramatic enemy attack.

    **b** The words in bold have connotations of serious crime and mortal danger.

    **c** The italicised words in the passage create a sustained metaphor of mosquitoes and humans being enemies engaged in battle.

    **d** The rhetorical questions, imperative sentences and non-sentences add a sense of drama and urgency to the passage.

    **e** The use of *we* makes the assumption that the reader has had the same experiences and shares the writer's hostile feelings towards mosquitoes

**3** **a** *raise* is a regular transitive verb (requiring an object) meaning to put something in a higher position, e.g. *He raised his head*

      *rise* is an irregular intransitive verb meaning to put oneself in a higher position, e.g. *He rose from his bed*

      arise is an irregular intransitive verb meaning to occur, e.g. *An unforeseen problem arose.*

    **b** raise – raised – raised; rise – rose – risen; arise – arose – arisen.

**5** The first conditional uses the <u>present simple</u> tense with the future tense for events which are <u>probable</u>. Second conditionals, which use the simple past followed by <u>would</u> plus <u>the infinitive (without to)</u>, signify an event which could happen but which is <u>improbable</u>. Third conditionals, formed with the <u>past perfect</u> tense followed by <u>would have</u> plus <u>the past participle</u>, mean that the event is <u>impossible</u> because it is <u>too late</u>. There are also zero conditionals, using simple present in both clauses, which refer <u>to permanent truths</u>.

**7** **(Sample answers)**

    **i** we are not aware of them until too late

    **ii** they give the impression of celebrating victory

    **iii** they behave sneakily

    **iv** they bite/leave a painful swelling

    **v** they spread malaria

    **vi** we have to waste time dealing with them

    **vii** we have to make an effort to deal with them

    **viii** it costs money to deal with them

    **ix** they steal our blood

    **x** they are very difficult to kill

**8** (Answers may include)

- Mosquitoes are a carrier of a deadly disease which affects many parts of the world.
- Without protection, you may contract malaria, which can be fatal.
- The insects are small and may not be easily visible, so always be vigilant.
- Listen for the characteristic whining sound they make while flying.
- Keep all parts of your body covered when mosquitoes may be present.
- Sprays, coils, creams or nets should be used before settling to sleep at night.
- In some cases it may be advisable to take anti-malarial pills.
- Areas of standing water near your home should be drained or sprayed.

**10** (Sample answers)

*preternaturally* - inexplicably, abnormally; *perseveringly* - determinedly, tenaciously; *convulsively* - jerkily, twitchily; *vexation* - annoyance, irritation; *diverting* - distracting; *forebodings* - disquiet, unease, trepidation; *unwholesome* - unhealthy, harmful; *adorned* - decorated, furnished; *ruffian* - lout, hooligan; *astronomer* - scientific observer of the stars

**11** setting - unknown room, four-poster bed, stifling, unwholesome, dripping; dark old picture.

action - nervous, wide awake, fever; wondered; the repetition of *now* and list of futile actions in the first paragraph convey the writer's inability to sleep.

language - groaned, horrors, rack, forebodings, danger, suffering, terror, shading, intently, constraint, gloomy, sinister ruffian; desperado.

**12** (Sample answers)

**a** After having realised he would not be able to sleep, the narrator looked around the room.

**b** Before noticing the picture, the narrator studied the furniture.

**c** Not only could the narrator not sleep, but he was also frightened.

**d** Even though he tried his pillow in several positions, he could not find a comfortable one.

**e** In spite of the moonlight and the candle glow, the narrator could not see the picture clearly.

# Unit 11

**2** **(Sample answers)**

  **a** moving fast

  **b** favoured with

  **c** suffering from

  **d** supreme achievement

  **e** from the beginning

  **f** going towards

  **g** more than

  **h** say no to

  **i** best part

  **j** difficult to improve on

**3** **(Sample answer)**

The world-renowned IceHotel is a completely new experience in holiday travel and accommodation. Not only is the beauty of the snowy Scandinavian landscape all around you, with its unique winter sports, but you get the experience of actually living in it. Yes, the IceHotel is actually made of ice, and so are many of the things in it. But no, it isn't cold! The world's largest frozen palace is cosy and welcoming, and all the thermal wear you need is provided.

After a day being driven in a sledge pulled by huskies, or cross-country skiing - or even lassoing reindeer – you can return to the warmth of your fur-covered ice bed. If you prefer, you can take a snowmobile and overnight in a wilderness cabin with steaming sauna.

Every winter the hotel is built again, so it's always new.

You'll have plenty of tales to tell your friends when you get home!

**6** **(Some examples of suitable points )**

  • After waking up from a deep sleep – because by night-time I feel so exhausted, because of the non-stop work and because the cold takes it out of you – we had a long meeting about the expedition in which we organised our food rations for the weeks ahead.

  • Despite our breakfast consisting of granola and oats, lunch of carbohydrate bars, soup and nuts, and dinner of pasta or rice, we also somehow have to eat a block of butter a day to keep our energy levels up.

  • This afternoon I went to build an igloo with Simon, one of the three Inuit hunters with our party, having killed his first polar bear when he was six, who is great because he's got a true sense of humour and I feel safer having him around, since he knows the environment well.

126

7   (Sample answer)

Questions, exclamations and direct speech convey the drama of the situation and Sam's panic. (Polar bears have already been mentioned on 23rd April as something to cause frissons of fear.) The action is interspersed with description of the bear to slow the narrative pace; mist and light are mentioned to create mysteriousness, as if the bear has supernatural power; short paragraphs convey the idea of events happening quickly and out of control; live ammunition is referred to, and even the cracker shells are enough to kill a person; the bear is moving aggressively towards them (charged) with real purpose. The fact that the bear was hungry, didn't scare easily, and was as big as they get – a full-grown male bear – all add to the threat posed by the animal.

8   (Sample answers)

- Was the temperature a problem?
- Did you feel lonely?
- What did you have to eat?
- What were the dangers?
- What was your most frightening experience on the trip?
- What was the food like?
- Did you have local Inuits with the party?
- What was your best experience on the trip?
- What are the dangers of trekking across snowy landscape?
- Why are you so concerned about what is happening in the Arctic?
- How has global warming affected the Arctic?

10  (Sample answer)

a   Sam enjoyed the peacefulness of the place, the beautiful scenery and the magnificent wild life, as well as the company and skills of the Inuit.

b   He was concerned about the effects of global warming in the area, which include a high rate of UV radiation, the melting ice, hungry animals (because of the population decline of the prey and increased competition among predatory species), and the threat to both the livelihood of the Inuit hunters and to the planet as a whole.

# Unit 12

**2** **a** The first two are not real words and the third is a kind of quotation.

    **b** The first is a foreign word and the second is a film title.

**3** **(Sample answer)**

The four questions in Passage **A** are a rhetorical device to engage the reader in the dilemma, practical and moral, of resurrecting extinct species. They show the scepticism of the writer towards this project, and his belief that animals should not be allowed to become extinct in the first place.

**5** **(Sample answers)**

    **a** told the world – announced

    **b** wiped from the face of the planet – exterminated

    **c** tracked down – discovered

    **d** basis of the plot – storyline

    **e** the stuff of science fiction – fantasy

**6** **Points to include:**

What scientists have already achieved: a sheep was cloned; DNA was collected from the last *bucardo*; embryos were created; they were implanted; a *bucardo* was born in 2003.

What they would like to achieve: bringing back a recently extinct Australian frog; resurrection of famous long-extinct animals.

**9** **(Sample answers)**

    **a** DNA is cellular molecule carrying genetic code which determines human behaviour and characteristics. The ladders of this double-helix-shaped molecule consist of nucleotides, of which we have 3 billion in our bodies. These genetic markers, almost all of them individual – except for close relatives and identical twins – form the basis of testing. Because all cells contain the same DNA, test samples can be taken from anywhere in the body.

    **b** The continuous prose is in the style of an article, whereas you would expect to find bullet points for easy reference in a science textbook or on an information website.